To
Claire
Best Wishes
Arte

AITCH: A LIFE IN COLOUR

*A donation from the sale of this book will be made to the
Sickle Cell Society.*

AITCH:
A LIFE IN
COLOUR

JILL KING

Matador
9 Priory Business Park
Kibworth Beauchamp
Leicestershire LE8 0RX, UK
Tel: (+44) 116 279 2299
Fax: (+44) 116 279 2277
Email: books@troubador.co.uk
Web: www.troubador.co.uk/matador

ISBN:
SB: 978-1783062-065
HB: 978-1783062-072

British Library Cataloguing in Publication Data.
A catalogue record for this book is available from the British Library.

Typeset in Aldine by Troubador Publishing Ltd
Printed and bound in the UK by TJ International, Padstow, Cornwall

Matador is an imprint of Troubador Publishing Ltd

aitch Petow

Artiste
Cutter
supreme

"Who helped name the scissors", and
as a colleage and friend over
20 yrs. you have gained every bodys
respect, love and admiration. —

me too
Vidal Vidal Sassoon

Aitch Peters is a leading creative hair stylist who has been at the top of his professional craft for 40 years. He is also an accomplished artist.

In this book his extraordinary life is explored through a series of conversations with Jill King, one of his regular clients at the Sassoon salon in the City of London. Their conversations – lively, funny and at times shocking – tell Aitch's inspirational story from his humble beginnings in Dominica to a life of creativity, glamour and adventure.

Aitch's stories reveal the connections between the craft of hairdressing and the artistic spirit in all its forms from ballet to cooking.

While Aitch and Jill appear at first to have very little in common, they come to appreciate and respect the similarities in their professional experiences, and in their personal values, as their relationship develops.

About the author

Jill King has had a highly successful professional career in the City for over 30 years and was the HR director at Linklaters, a leading global law firm, from 2005 to 2012. She is a business writer and commentator on the professions.

CONTENTS

Foreword   x

A Most Unlikely Couple   1

And the Winner Is…   9

My Sweet Sugar Mandy   27

Sculpture in Motion   37

City of Angels?   55

French Lessons   69

Art on a Plate   81

My Grandmother's Wisdom   89

Conquering Fears   103

Son of a Preacher Man   111

In the Psychiatrist's Chair   123

Decadence, Sleaze and Excess   135

East of Harlesden   147

The Artist Within   159

Homage   167

Full Circle   175

Acknowledgements   182

Aitch: A Career in Highlights   185

FOREWORD

There are many celebrities famous enough to be referred to by just one name. One would never need to refer to Madonna by anything other than her Christian name. Utter the name Coco and one immediately knows that it is Chanel that it is being discussed; Elvis, Marilyn etc., the list goes on. Modern day pop stars such as J. Lo and Jay-Z have taken the process one step further and have abbreviated their names down to truncated initials. There is, however, only one person that I am aware of that is known simply by one letter… 'H'.

I first witnessed the talent and showmanship of Aitch when I had been at Sassoon just a few months. He won the Sassoon Inter Salon Soiree with a beautiful presentation of stunning models sashaying down the catwalk to 'La Vie En Rose' by Grace Jones; it was totally mesmerising and totally Aitch! For months afterwards, you couldn't walk into a Sassoon salon anywhere without hearing this being played.

My next significant encounter with Aitch was when I was made his junior in London's South Molton Street. At the time, Sassoon creative directors were impossibly flamboyant and full of exotic characters, with Aitch possibly the most flamboyant creative director of all. The juniors had been polishing and cleaning the salon in readiness for the senior team and the first clients' arrival, usually at 9am. However, Aitch didn't arrive with the rest of the team and as the minutes become an hour, and his well-heeled clientele arriving, there was still no sign of Aitch. Of course, this was before mobile phones, so I just had to appease his clients as best as I could and wait…

✂ *x* ✂

All of a sudden, there was a commotion at the desk as Aitch made his entrance, a flurry of Louis Vuitton luggage, Maxfield Parrish floor-length fur coat, YSL shoes, suit, sunglasses (whatever the weather) and a haze of Grey Flannel cologne. Sauntering over to the trio of clients (and handing me the coat and luggage without missing a step), he pronounced to each client in turn, "Darling you simply must have a treatment... colour... perm... before we start." All were instantly assuaged by his gentle, polite, charming, and ever so slightly risqué charisma, and they of course always dutifully complied. Well, Aitch knew best, didn't he...?

I was lucky enough to assist Aitch whenever he was out on shoots or fashion shows, and later in my career being part of the team that accompanied him on the numerous hair shows he conducted around the world.

That was the way it was with Aitch, each day was a carnival of models, celebrities, shoots, and shows, always hectic, always exciting and always fun. Like the list above, there will only ever be one Marilyn or one Elvis; there will, as well, certainly only ever be one Aitch!

Mark Hayes
International Creative Director
Sassoon

In a word, then, learn to fascinate.

Villiers David,
Advice to my Godchildren

A MOST UNLIKELY COUPLE

A-I-T-C-H. I had to ask the receptionist to spell it out for me in the end with a mixture of exasperation and disbelief at my end of the phone. Why was it that hair stylists had to have such ridiculous names? Were they born with them or did they just adopt them to make themselves sound more creative?

By now, I was used to booking appointments with stylists with names like Tamzin or Florien, but this really was the most ridiculous one I'd come across. I didn't even know whether Aitch was a man or a woman, and by the time I'd asked the receptionist to repeat the name three times, it seemed impertinent to ask any more questions. But I was off to Brazil that day on a four-day business trip and my hair desperately needed cutting – so I took the slot that was offered, and just hoped that the experience of 'Aitch' cutting my hair would be over quickly so that I could get on my way to the airport.

To be honest, I've never enjoyed going to the hairdressers. I've always been rather self-conscious about my looks, never being a pretty child, and a bit of a tomboy when I was young. I used to love riding my bicycle, building dens and climbing trees. At school I was studious, and more interested in books than fashion or make-up.

So sitting for nearly an hour in front of a mirror at the hairdressers had never been a pleasure, it felt more like a form of torture to me. I certainly didn't relish the expectation there always seemed to be that I'd sit and chat breezily as my hair was being cut. I'd always found these conversations rather false and predictable, however hard the stylist tried to be friendly. I didn't want to tell Tamzin or Florien about my holidays or my weekend, and I was never convinced they were really that interested; it just seemed like a ritual.

To me, going to the salon was a chore, something that needed to be done, and I just wanted my hair cut efficiently so that I could get out of there as soon as possible. But right now, I really did need a haircut. It had been nearly two months since I'd last subjected myself to a visit to the hairdressers, and I knew I couldn't leave it any longer.

I had at least found a new salon that I'd started to visit fairly regularly – Sassoon in the City. I'd picked up Vidal Sassoon's autobiography once in an airport bookshop and read it on a long plane journey. I admired the way he'd built a successful business empire, and I was fascinated by the way Bauhaus architecture of all things had inspired him to create the iconic Sassoon styles of the 1960s. I was impressed by the way he'd invested in his staff and created a highly regarded academy where stylists were trained, not just for his own company, but for the hairdressing industry as a whole. I appreciated these weren't typical reasons for choosing a salon, but the Sassoon brand somehow struck a chord, despite the hairdressing world being so alien to me.

I checked my watch and sighed as I put my papers together for my trip. It was time to go so I grabbed my bag and walked down the corridor to the lift. I enjoyed doing business internationally but it was exhausting. I knew however that if my hair was cut professionally, and if I felt it looked good, I would be more confident. It was a bit of a performance really, and looking good was a key part of it all, whether I liked it or not.

I jumped in a cab and arrived at the Sassoon salon in a matter of minutes. It was a square building with large windows and a modest façade. It struck me that architecturally the style was reminiscent of Bauhaus, but I realised this similarity must have been purely coincidental. The décor inside was bright and contemporary but with a touch of class and without being too trendy for more mature clients like me. As you arrived there were a couple of steps down to the reception area on the left and the welcome was always friendly and polite. I enjoyed the few moments of reflection I usually had sitting on the sofa waiting for a stylist to appear.

The receptionist took my coat and bag and I put on one of those dreadful nylon gowns they insist you wear at hairdressing salons. The gowns at the Sassoon salon were brown and as shapeless as any I'd encountered, with the usual Velcro fastenings and baggy sleeves. They reminded me of hospital gowns that I'd always thought made even the healthiest of patients look sad and vulnerable. It was strange really that no one had come up with a more stylish solution for a hairdressing salon.

I was ushered to a position and reluctantly looked at myself in the mirror. There were dark shadows under my eyes and my hair looked flat and lifeless. I reflected on the fact that I'd always struggled to have a distinctive style. As a student, I'd had long hair with a central parting and I'd kept it like that for years, just tying it back for work.

Then when I reached thirty, I took the bold step – for me at least – of having a fringe cut for the first time. I kept that hairstyle right up until my 40th birthday when I was persuaded it was time to have a shorter style and had it cut into a classic bob. When I looked back, it seemed as though every ten years I felt the need to change my hairstyle. The bob wasn't a great success, to be honest. I was too impatient to give the blow-drying the time or respect it needed, and my hair would hang limply with little of the sharp shape it was meant to have. My best friend Philomena despaired of me and often insisted on blow-drying my hair herself.

At least my hair hadn't gone grey, even though I was now in my early 50s. I said a little prayer of thanks to my late father who hadn't had a single grey hair right into his early 60s. I could only imagine that it was from him that I'd inherited that particular gene. I would be forever grateful to him for that, not least because it meant I'd never had to subject myself to the ritual of regularly colouring my hair. I sighed quietly to myself at that thought, and settled into my seat.

Just then I looked up and saw a stylist approaching me in the mirror. Somehow I knew instantly who it was. He was tall, very elegant, immaculately dressed, extraordinarily stylish – someone who made an immediate impact and demanded attention. He was wearing a soft linen jacket in a subtle shade of peach with the sleeves turned up, showing off a designer watch with a large round face and a silver wristband. His shirt was tapered and fitted him perfectly with beautifully crafted horn buttons. And his black low-slung trousers, with embroidered pockets, were held perfectly in place by a huge Hermès belt – so, this was Aitch. He moved with grace and held his head high, not with arrogance but with quiet self-confidence. His presence filled the room with authority. I could tell he was very aware of his surroundings, of the clients and of the juniors, and that he had an unspoken respect for them all. He made a beeline for me, and in the instant that he spoke, I was conscious of him giving me his full attention.

"Hi Jill," he said. "I'm Aitch, how are you today?" He spoke in a deep gentle voice with a melodic lilt. And he smelt divine, not over-powering, but with a subtle fragrance that hinted of a man who paid attention to every detail of his appearance. We talked briefly about my hair and what I wanted.

"Just tidy it up and make it a little shorter," I said, a little more briskly than I'd meant to, but mentally thinking to myself – *short enough that I don't need to come back here again too soon*. Aitch didn't press me for more instructions; he just put his fingers through my hair to assess it, and smiled warmly in a way that reassured me he wouldn't do anything too drastic.

"For sure," he said, and before I knew it I was whisked away to the sink area for my obligatory hair wash with one of the assistants.

To my surprise, as I leaned my head back on the rim of the cold sink and felt the hot water on my scalp, my mind was buzzing with thoughts about Aitch. He certainly wasn't what I'd expected. He was of an uncertain age, but he had the confident air that comes with years of experience, and I felt instantly at ease with him. This wasn't a young stylist who'd make me feel middle-aged and frumpy, or someone I could instantly tell I didn't have anything in common with. He was naturally flamboyant but in a refined classy sort of way; he'd sparked my curiosity, and despite my prejudices about hairdressers I somehow couldn't dismiss him as frivolous or showy. I relaxed as the young assistant gently massaged my hair and I wished, as I always did, that this part of the process at least would last a bit longer. But in a flash I was up again, with a towel wrapped precariously around my head, sitting in front of mirror waiting for Aitch to return.

We started to talk, a little tentatively at first. I mentioned that I was off to the airport to travel to Sao Paulo for a few days on business. We chatted about Brazil and the joys and challenges of international travel. Aitch was extremely knowledgeable, and took a keen interest in what I had to say. He talked about places he'd been to as well, and it was soon clear that these weren't just the usual European cities and holiday resorts; he'd travelled to some pretty exotic and unlikely parts of the world such as Tokyo, South Korea and the Philippines. It wasn't clear to me when or why he'd travelled so extensively, but I could tell that there was a lot more to Aitch than met the eye.

Despite the fact that we were talking to each other's reflection in the mirror, I felt his warm attention to everything I was saying and I started to lose a little of my self-consciousness as I focused on Aitch and what he had to say.

He asked me questions that were sincere and informed – how did I cope with the cultural differences? And how did travelling to Brazil compare with travelling to South East Asia?

Before I knew it, I found myself engaged in the sort of

conversation I'd not experienced before with a hair stylist. I prided myself on how well travelled I was. I even kept a running list of all the countries I'd visited, and I had an on-going competition with my husband Mike about which of us had been to the most places. While Aitch didn't show off about his own experiences, it was pretty clear he could give me a run for my money when it came to the far-flung places he'd been to, and I could tell he and I were capable of a much deeper conversation than the ones I normally associated with a hairdressing salon.

As Aitch went about his work, I put my BlackBerry away and started to pay more attention to him. His curiosity in me was infectious, and I found myself observing him carefully, wondering what experiences or secrets might lie beneath his professional demeanour. I noticed a hand-stitched name tag on his scissors case with a huge letter 'H' embroidered on it. Aitch was very attentive and saw me glance at it. He picked it up and handed it to me.

"That was made for me by one of my clients," he said, smiling warmly. "I keep my favourite scissors in it."

As I held the tag in my hand and admired the close detail of the stitching, I was surprised and impressed by what it implied. A client giving such a personalised gift clearly spoke of a deeper relationship between hair stylist and client than I was used to, and I was touched by Aitch's trusting willingness to share the story behind it with me. This was a man clearly loved by his clients, and who, I could tell, was at ease with himself and confident in his craft.

All too soon, my haircut was finished and Aitch was holding up the mirror behind my head for me to see it for myself. The haircut looked great and for once I was sorry it was over. I wanted to know more about Aitch. He intrigued me. *Who was this man who could have had such an impact? What was the source of his inner confidence that shone through so clearly? And where did that name come?*

It would all have to wait. I had a plane to catch.

What you do is live, and life must begin from within. Everything in life is purposeful.

Acts of Faith, Iyania Vanzan

AND THE WINNER IS...

For once in my life, I was actually looking forward to going to the hairdressers, but not for any of the normal reasons. I wasn't rushing to the salon to get a new look or to have a haircut to make myself feel better. My anticipation was all about meeting Aitch again. He'd been on my mind since I'd first met him. Of all the people I'd met in my life, very few had made such an immediate impact on me.

As I walked into the salon again, I felt a frisson of nervous anticipation. *What if the experience wasn't the same this time? Had I imagined what had seemed like a special aura around this guy?* Well, I would soon find out I decided, as I announced my arrival to the receptionist. I sat down and waited.

After a few minutes, one of the young assistants helped me into the nylon cutting gown, and I was ushered to one of the stylist positions and offered a drink. I asked for a glass of water thinking it might help my nerves, and tried to breathe slowly and keep calm. I could feel my heart beating a little faster than normal. It was an odd and unexpected feeling. I was known for being cool and unflappable, and the idea that meeting my hair stylist was making me feel nervous was a little unsettling.

Just when my nerve came close to faltering, I saw him in the mirror. There was a lower floor where the stylists spent their rest periods with a wide sweeping staircase, which led up from there to the salon floor. As I watched in the mirror, each of the stylists would emerge behind me to meet their clients and it reminded me of a musical conductor rising to the podium to meet the audience and start a performance. As Aitch stepped into the main salon, his arrival had the same sense of authority and anticipation that I'd experienced at the start of a concert. He was wielding scissors rather than a baton, but he was in total command of his surroundings, and ready to perform.

Today he was wearing a white fitted shirt with patterned cuffs under an electric blue Versace jacket with gold buttons on the sleeves. He sported a silk yellow and blue Hermès scarf around his neck with a matching silk handkerchief in his top pocket. His oblong black Italian designer glasses made him look interesting and intelligent, and his tall slim frame was flattered by his blue skinny jeans and extravagantly wide leather belt. He looked fabulous and he knew it.

"Hello Jill," he beamed, "so lovely to see you again."

And I could tell from his tone and his smile that he really meant it and that, much to my relief, I hadn't been wrong. There really was something about Aitch that was different and special. I was hoping to find out more, but first we had to talk about my hair.

"It's held its shape well," said Aitch, running his fingers gently through the top of my head. "But I think we could make it slightly sharper this time".

I agreed without hesitation. I had an instinctive feeling that whatever Aitch had in mind for my hair, he'd make me look good. I'd had loads of compliments since the first haircut he'd given me and that had already done wonders for my confidence in how I looked.

I was ushered over to the row of washbasins to have my hair washed, but I was impatient to get back to the chair where I would hear more from Aitch. I knew we weren't going to be talking about weekend plans and holidays like everyone else, and it felt like a guilty secret. I sat back in the chair with a towel on my head, and then Aitch reappeared with his scissors and put his hands on my shoulders. His gentle touch relaxed me and made a reconnection between us.

From our first encounter, I expected we'd pick up our conversation about international travel and I wasn't disappointed. Aitch had remembered our discussion, and asked me about my recent trip to Brazil. "It went well, thank you," I said, but I wanted to hear about all the places he'd been to, so I didn't lose any time in asking him about his own travels.

"I've been to lots of amazing places, Jill," he began, in answer to my questioning, "but Los Angeles was a special place for me because I lived there and discovered it for myself. It's somewhere that's had a big impact on my life."

"What were you doing there?" I asked.

"Well, Jill," Aitch replied, "I was lucky enough to be asked to work for Vidal Sassoon in the Beverly Hills salon, and I ended up living in California for many years."

"What sort of impact did it have on you?" I asked, curious to find out more.

"As soon as I arrived there," he said, "I loved everything about it, from the early bird parking, to the way you could get absolutely anything you wanted delivered to your apartment at any time of day or night – even marijuana," he laughed, looking at me quizzically in the mirror as if to judge my reaction.

"I simply fell in love with the place," he continued. "It had a real sense of urgency and a buzz that was exciting and infectious. It was a 24/7 city that rarely slept, a place where limousines were as standard as buses, and of course, it was extremely glamorous. In fact, it opened up a whole new lifestyle for me."

"What do you mean?" I asked, genuinely curious.

"Before I knew it," he replied, "I found myself adopting the way they did things over there and mixing with celebrities. I remember the very first time I attended to Faye Dunaway for example," he said, his voice trailing off a little as if summoning up an image buried deep in his memory bank, "and how star-struck I felt at the time."

I was listening intently to his every word, but even so I couldn't be sure I'd heard him correctly. Did he mean *the* Faye Dunaway? I tried not to look too surprised, but I wanted to know more.

"So, how did that come about?" I asked.

"Well," Aitch continued, clearly pleased with my interest in his story, "Terry O' Neill, who I'd worked with as a session stylist in London, and who was Faye's husband at the time, rang me one day to say that she was coming over to Los Angeles from New York and didn't know any stylists out there. He asked me to do her hair and to find a make-up artist for a photo session that *L.A. Style* magazine were organising as they were running a feature on her.

"So I got my people to speak to her people," he tittered, winking at me in the mirror, "and we met up in the studio. She wanted a real girl-next-door look with plenty of volume in her hair, and it was my job to make that happen.

"Back in London," he went on, "I'd worked with lots of leading photographers, such as David Bailey and Lord Lichfield, so I was well groomed in how to work with famous models and actresses. It gave me the confidence I needed to work with Faye Dunaway, especially as I was a huge fan of hers."

"How interesting, and what was it like working with such a big name?" I asked, desperately trying to remember the films that Faye Dunaway had starred in.

"Well, in fact," Aitch replied, "that first encounter in the studio led to me spending six full days with her in her luxury suite at the Beverly Hills Hotel."

"Wow," I said, gushing uncharacteristically, "that must have been amazing." My mind was full of questions, but I couldn't stop myself from asking the obvious one, "What she like in real life?"

"She was a megastar," said Aitch, smiling knowingly, "an icon of the time – she was immersed in a kind of celebrity galaxy, a cocoon where her every need or want was served on demand. It was 1988, and she was over in L.A. promoting the film *Barfly* that she starred in with Mickey Rourke. It explored the morality and demise of an alcoholic and was quite a talking point at the time. Of course, I realise now that it was confronting a really important subject, but I didn't really get it back then. I was more interested in meeting Faye, and wrapped up in the show business of it all – and I was so delighted for her when she won the Golden Globe award for Best Actress.

"You see, Jill," Aitch continued, "Faye was one of my all-time favourite actresses. I first saw her at the cinema when she played the lead actress in *Bonnie and Clyde*, and later on I went to see her in *The Thomas Crown Affair* and *Eyes of Laura Mars*. She was world-famous, a true femme fatale, and there I was, up close and personal with her – I couldn't believe I was in the same room as her and kept pinching myself to make sure it wasn't all a dream. I was just massively excited, but I had to be professional and not let that show."

"What was her luxury suite like?" I asked.

"Well," Aitch replied excitedly, "as I walked in, all I could see was a sea of shoes on the floor; there was designer luggage everywhere, and her amazing wardrobe was draped on every piece of furniture. There was a sitting room with a mirrored dressing table over-flowing with stockings and all the rudimentary necessities a mega-star requires. There was even a drawer reserved solely for her collection of designer sunglasses. She smoked continuously at the time but without ever finishing a cigarette. She'd lean back languidly on the sofa while she was being attended to, take a few puffs on her cigarette and then proceed to stub it out while starting another straightaway.

"It was like a scene out of one of her movies, Jill – complete and utter decadence – and I had a front row seat. I watched it all just like it was my own private performance."

There was a certain triumph in his voice as Aitch paused to concentrate more fully on cutting the left side of my hair, and I could tell he was enjoying reliving the whole experience as he worked.

"She spoke in a low voice," Aitch continued, moving across to my right-hand side, "and she had a tone that implied 'don't mess with me'. She knew exactly what she wanted, but she was understated with a kind of studied glamour." It was obvious that Aitch had been mesmerised by her, but that he'd dealt with the situation with great respect and poise. "Her make-up took hours to complete," he went on, "but she didn't look made up at all by the end of it, just naturally very beautiful. She knew her best angle and how to enhance or embellish it, and she always wanted to look her best."

I could picture Aitch right there, watching, observing and honing his skills. I wondered which other glamorous women he'd worked with in L.A., and what lessons he'd learnt from them about how to make a woman feel good.

Before I could ask him, Aitch continued telling his story.

"I also attended to Faye when she was preparing to go to the Oscar awards ceremony," he said. "We started really early that day – there was a lot to get through with her make-up and hair to be done, and her choice of designer gown to be made. Faye was at the centre of it all of course, walking around in her dressing gown with a cigarette in her hand, rollers in her hair, and only half made up. There was this enormous rack of exquisite gowns in her hotel suite that had been lent to her by a string of designers. I'd never seen anything like it, and the chaos of it all was more like a scene from a house-move than a designer fashion show. Faye would hold one gown up after another and Dala, the make-up artist, and I would be asked to give our opinion. We would tell her how the gown went with her skin tone and what we proposed for her make-up and hair to suit the style of each one.

"In fact," he continued, "she always ended up choosing to have her hair down, and I knew that was what would happen, but it was all part of the routine, and we talked her through all the other options. We wanted her to look like a goddess. After a while she would narrow the choice down, and we would lay a couple of gowns on the bed with all the accessories, shoes and jewellery we thought would go best with each of them. Then a final choice would be made – with our approval, of course," he laughed.

I could imagine the scene, and Aitch needed little prompting to tell me more. "In those days the Oscars were held downtown at the Shrine Auditorium," he explained, "and the event started at three o'clock in the afternoon. To get there in time, Faye had to be picked up from her hotel at noon, so it was a really hectic morning. Just before she left for the ceremony, a cavalcade of trolleys were wheeled down the corridor and brought ceremoniously into her suite. They were piled high with linen napkins, crystal cut champagne glasses and Beluga caviar served on ice, with blinis, eggs, crème fraiche and finely chopped scallions.

"By this time, the room was full of her friends and her invited guests, but none of them drank very much; they just sipped champagne and stood around looking gorgeous. Dala and I watched, totally fascinated, as they sampled a little caviar. Then they put on their finest fur coats and evening stoles and left in their limos."

"How extraordinary," I exclaimed, "So you and Dala were left there alone in her suite once they'd all gone?"

"Precisely," said Aitch, with a telling grin. "But even better than that, as Faye made her grand exit, she turned around, looked us both in the eye and pointing to the champagne and canapés said, 'Help yourselves darlings.'"

"So that's how I ended up spending Oscar night in a star's luxury hotel suite," said Aitch. "Dala and I drank champagne all night long and gorged ourselves on the fabulous food, and on the whole situation we found ourselves in. We luxuriated on the huge double bed, propped up by the finest white down pillows and watched the Oscar ceremony on an enormous TV with glasses of Dom Pérignon in our hands. Over the course of the evening we slowly demolished the towers of caviar between us, squealing at the sight of every celebrity as they appeared on the red carpet. We felt like royalty."

Just at that moment, Aitch's next client arrived and he went to greet her. I watched as he glided across the room and gave her his full attention. I was left reeling. Who'd have guessed that Aitch had worked with clients like Faye Dunaway, and with photographers as famous as Terry O'Neill? I loved the quiet modesty with which he'd told me the story and I could easily see how his humility had endeared him to the rich and famous. I sensed that these experiences had in some way developed his professional sensibilities, but how all of this had come about was unclear.

Aitch came back smiling and I knew there was more he wanted to tell me. "Of course Jill", he went on, "I attended the Oscar ceremony myself a couple of times after that."

"Did you really?" I said, trying to disguise my disbelief.

"Yes I did actually," Aitch replied. "On the first occasion, I was invited backstage to work with Debbie Allen. She was a leading Hollywood producer and choreographer at the time, and had become a client of mine at the Beverly Hills salon. She was choreographing the Oscars that year, and I was attending to her, so I was given a pass that gave me access to all the backstage areas. Debbie was a really big personality – and I was in tow as it were," Aitch said, brimming with pride and putting his hands on his hips. "She had a killer make-up artist and we worked together as part of her personal team. Everything was designed to allow her to get on with her job without worrying about her appearance."

"Tell me more," I said.

"Oscar night, as you can imagine Jill, was a real high octane event – a pumped up ten-megawatt situation, you might say. I had to learn to develop my own positive energy and to sustain it through the rehearsals for all the lighting cues and entrances and exits that went on for hours. I also learnt to be discrete. I was in constant attendance to Debbie and she trusted me to make sure there wasn't a hair out of place or any shine on her face. I realised early on that it was important to reassure her that she looked great, so I regularly punctuated what I was doing with carefully timed and sincere compliments. It was an amazing experience, everything was provided, and anyone who was anyone darling," he said, slowly rolling his eyes, "had their own personal assistant." We both smiled and I pictured the scene, with hordes of self-important assistants fussing around the celebrities like bees around a honey pot.

"Of course, there was a lot of curiosity about me and my strange accent," Aitch said, smiling broadly. "I was constantly being asked if I was a cockney," he laughed. "An English accent in Hollywood was pretty unusual in those days, and everyone assumed that if you were English, you had to be a cockney. But actually it made me stand out and be remembered, and that was really important in L.A.

"I remember an encounter with Patti Labelle in her trailer once. She had a huge bucket of KFC in her lap, and was fascinated to meet a black guy from London speaking proper English – 'innit!' We both laughed as Aitch put on a mock cockney voice. "Since then of course I've perfected my accent," he said, "it's a sort of mix of cockney and Essex with elements of slang from da hood, and a dash of Stacey Solomon – Oh my God!" he exclaimed loudly and with attitude.

"You said you'd been to the Oscars on a couple of occasions," I reminded him, keen to hear more.

"Yes, Jill," he replied. "The following year I was asked to do the hair of one of the Oscar's design team along with Kathy one of the Sassoon colour technicians, and we were both given invitations to the awards ceremony. I spent days preparing myself for it. I loved all of that. Of course it was important that I looked the part, so I had a beautifully tailored tuxedo made for me by Cecilia Lamb, and I wore a black bowtie and a black cummerbund. My white dress shirt was pristine and it had gold cherub studs down the front. I dressed it with my favourite diamond and crystal cufflinks from Phillips of London." Aitch stood up straight and beamed at me in the mirror. "I looked very handsome," he said, not arrogantly but with a quiet personal pride. "It was a true moment of assured ego for me."

"How did you get to the ceremony?" I asked.

"Well, Jill, I knew the traffic would be gridlocked that day and it would take around two and a half hours to reach the auditorium," Aitch replied, "so everything was planned in great detail. I arranged to be picked up in a limo and was driven there in what became a snaking line of white stretch limos – it was just like circling to land at Heathrow as we got closer," he laughed. "There were banks of photographers stacked on either side of the red carpet, like high-rise buildings forming a corridor that we walked along to reach the entrance."

"As I made my way down the red carpet, I felt like Denzel Washington," Aitch said proudly. "I'd always wanted to be an actor when I was younger, but that wasn't something my family were ever going to allow. Yet here I was living my dream. I remember the exotic smell of the extravagant flower displays that lined the red carpet. The fragrance was wonderfully abundant even though we were outside – I hadn't expected that, and the power of it knocked me back. The whole experience made me feel as though time was passing very slowly, and I savoured every moment of it – I thought I'd well and truly arrived. All that scrubbing and detailed planning I'd put into presenting myself had paid off."

Aitch smiled broadly and looked pleased with himself as he reflected on the memory. "The boy did good," he said.

I was stunned. I didn't know anyone who'd actually been to the Oscars and here was Aitch my hairdresser, who'd been twice, relaying the experience to me as if it was commonplace. "As I walked into the auditorium," he continued, "the ushers showed us to our seats and all I could see was a sea of tuxedos. The room was brimming with duchess satin and brocade and delicate evening shoes like slippers embellished with satin bows of all shapes and sizes."

I was starting to appreciate what an eye Aitch had for observation. He'd taken it all in, right down to the texture of the fabrics and the trimmings on each outfit. He had a gift for absorbing the essence of a scene, the colours and smells and the smallest of details, and recalling it all in full Technicolor in his mind's eye. I wondered where this capacity had come from, but Aitch was in full flow and I didn't want to interrupt his story.

"I sat in my seat feeling like a celebrity," he said. "I watched Whoopi Goldberg receive the Oscar for Best Supporting Actress in *Ghost*. She was only the second black actress to win an acting Oscar – the first one was Hattie McDaniel years earlier in *Gone with the Wind*. Patrick Swayze and Demi Moore were both there alongside her, and I felt strangely proud. After the show, there was the most spectacular fireworks display. The sky lit up as if the whole of Los Angeles was on fire."

"What did you do next?" I asked, curious to know how Aitch had partied the night away.

"Well Jill," he said, "we went for dinner at one of my favourite restaurants and had a sumptuous meal and masses of great champagne. By then I was on fire – I felt really hot – so I dumped Kathy back at the hotel and set out on an adventure all of my own. I took on the stretch limo solo as it were and cruised around the darker side of Hollywood with my personal driver until the early hours of the morning. I really made the most of the situation; dressed in black tie, full of the Oscar experience and with an excess of champagne in my veins. I was fuelled with sinful intent," he said, looking at me over his glasses in the mirror with a wicked smile, "and had the most amazing encounters with the most amazing people – you can't get more Hollywood than that!"

I decided not to try too hard imagining what decadence had gone on in the back of that limo. I wasn't about to ask him right there in the salon. He'd told me just enough for me to tell that he'd lived the experience to the full, and that it was a night he'd remember for the rest of his life.

I was reeling a bit from Aitch's stories, and trying desperately to organise my thoughts. There were so many things I wanted to know. He'd explained to me how he'd first met Faye Dunaway, and how he'd been to the Oscars, but how come he was mixing in such high-profile circles? I had to ask him.

Aitch didn't need much prompting. "It all started when I was invited to do a shoot in the desert," he said, with a playful laugh.

"I'm sorry?" I replied, struggling to understand what he was talking about.

"Well, Jill," he continued more seriously, "when I was working at Vidal Sassoon in London, I was invited to do an editorial shoot over in California for *Honey* magazine. I'd worked for the magazine before and I'd become a bit of a favourite of the editor Nicky Williams. Nicky was quite a character to tell the truth. She always wore Petruli – it's a kind of hippie scent with a particularly intoxicating smell and made her kind of hard to forget," said Aitch, pulling a face in the mirror.

"Anyway, I flew over to the States and was put up in a fabulous house that the magazine had rented for me in L.A. The shoot was taking place in Death Valley and every morning I'd get up really early and go for the most beautiful drive to get there. The colours of the landscape set against the morning sky were just stunning. That's when I really fell in love with the terrain and the special light they have in California.

"You have to remember Jill," he continued, "that London was a pretty drab place in the 80s, and I couldn't get over the sheer scale and the vibrancy of Los Angeles. I went shopping in Ralph's supermarket and literally gasped with delight when I saw the rows and rows of food all so extravagantly displayed, and at the tiny water sprinklers placed above the fruit and vegetables to keep them fresh. It was a place of rich abundance, and everything seemed amplified to me, larger than life."

It sounded like an amazing time but Aitch wasn't finished with his story just yet. "Mind you," he continued, "it was also in Death

Valley that I first experienced the kind of direct prejudice you used to get in the U.S."

"What do you mean?" I asked naively.

"Well Jill," he replied, patiently, "we all went into a bar after the shoot – me, the photographer, and a bevy of attractive models – and it was drinks all round. But the barman point blank refused to serve me."

"How did you deal with that?" I asked, a little shocked at the revelation.

"I wasn't on home territory and I didn't know how to react, so I just withdrew into myself and thankfully the team rallied round me as a sort of safety net. But that experience didn't change my dream to go back to L.A. and so, not long afterwards, when I was asked to be the creative director at the Vidal Sassoon salon in Beverly Hills, I jumped at the chance. Of course, it was hard at first contemplating leaving London and moving to the other side of the world, but I knew it was an opportunity I couldn't turn down. I'd just decorated my flat, and was actually feeling really settled at the time so I found it quite an ordeal planning such a colossal move away from my family, my friends and all my professional contacts. With my emotions running high, the only way I knew how to cope with my stress was to plan a farewell party – it gave me something to focus on, to distract me from all the upheaval of the move."

How typical of Aitch, I thought, as I listened to his story, *to party away his fears and anxieties.*

"Tell me about it," I said, knowing that Aitch was dying to describe it all to me.

"I was given permission by Annie Humphreys and Phillip Rogers, who were the managing directors of Sassoon at the time, to hold the party at the salon in Sloane Street – 44, Sloane Street – what an address for a party!" he said. "I organised it all myself, hiring a florist and caterers with waiters to serve the champagne and the canapés. I even had a doorman and a cloakroom attendant and a red carpet for my guests to walk on as they came in. There was a DJ who brought the whole atmosphere to life, and all in all the party was a massive success – and a very fitting farewell."

I could sense that Aitch was still very proud of what he had pulled off, and it was clearly a fond memory. "Looking back Jill," he said, "on all the detailing of the party, it was really a rehearsal for what I was to experience later on living in Hollywood."

"Tell me about that," I said, knowing he needed little prompting.

"I flew over from London and was taken by taxi to the L'Ermitage, a luxury hotel just a few steps away from Sunset Strip in West Hollywood," he explained. "I was put up by the company there while I settled in and looked for somewhere to live. As soon as I walked into the lobby of the hotel, I appreciated its sophisticated ambiance – and to my utter delight it was full of the most gorgeous looking guests. I felt immediately at home."

I could well imagine Aitch's pleasure on his arrival, but I wondered how easily he'd adjusted to the world of West Hollywood, and to his new life there, given how apprehensive he'd been about moving away from London.

Aitch was deep in thought. He started by recalling his early impressions of the hotel. "It was contemporary in style," he explained, "but in a classy sort of way with eclectic antiques from all over Europe. Of course, every possible thing a client might ask for was catered for – it even had a dining service for the guests' dogs." I raised my eyebrows, and Aitch nodded as if to dispel any disbelief in what I was hearing.

"I quickly discovered," he continued, "that the hotel also had a private wing with a separate entrance where certain guests would arrive in big sunglasses and hats. I didn't understand what was going on at first until another guest told me, in a whispered voice, that this was the place where celebrities came to stay after they'd had plastic surgery. They very rarely came out of their rooms as they wanted to stay hidden while their scars healed and their bandages were still on, so absolutely everything they ever wanted or needed was delivered to them by a butler."

I was getting the distinct impression that Aitch had had no trouble at all in adjusting to his new lifestyle in the States, and I smiled knowingly at him in the mirror.

"Once I knew that," he said with a grin, "I had a wonderful time perfecting the art of room service for myself. I ended up staying there for a whole month and ran up a huge bill by taking a taxi every day from the hotel to the salon on Rodeo Drive. I can also still remember the reams and reams of paper that made up my hotel bill when I checked out – every single thing I'd consumed had been itemised. I'd never seen anything like it – and I think the receptionist was a little surprised too," he said playfully, making me wonder what exactly Aitch had ordered from room service. From the pause in our conversation, it appeared he wasn't about to tell me.

"When was this?" I asked, trying to put these stories into some context.

"Well I arrived in L.A. in 1984, just a few weeks before the start of the Olympics that were held there," he said. "It was a very exciting time. Proctor and Gamble were one of the sponsors of the games and they'd built two hair salons just for the athletes. I worked there as part of the Vidal Sassoon team and we put together a new aerodynamic hair collection for the occasion. The salon actually became a bit of a mecca for the athletes. It was somewhere they could come without competition, a kind of tranquillity zone you might say. My own big moment came when I gave Florence Joyner-Kersee a Vidal Sassoon haircut in front of all the press. It made me very proud when I watched her go on to win three gold medals, two silvers and a bronze."

"So where did you end up living when you moved out of the hotel?" I asked.

"My first apartment was on the Kings Road and Santa Monica Boulevard," Aitch replied. "It was a small road with a local restaurant called Hugo's on the corner. It's famous for its breakfasts and I'd go there most mornings for eggs benedict served with homemade granary bread and freshly squeezed orange juice. It was a fabulous area to live in and I really enjoyed myself. I went to loads of parties and tried out all the gay bars in West Hollywood. In fact, it was in one of those bars that I first tried a Long Island Iced Tea, and it quickly became one of my favourite drinks."

I looked at Aitch quizzically. I'd heard of a Long Island Iced Tea and knew it was some sort of cocktail, but I'd never tried one myself.

"It's not that different to normal iced tea," Aitch joked, "except it's a bit more potent with seven spirits including vodka, rum, tequila, gin and triple sec with sour mix all topped off with coke, packed with ice and finished off with a lemon and mint garnish."

I felt a little drunk just listening to him reeling off the ingredients, and the detail in his description was absorbing. So much so I was barely aware of the salon surroundings.

By now Aitch was giggling in his charmingly playful way. "It was kind of 'hello, you want to get twished?' Then I'll have two of those please'. But quite frankly, even I could only manage two or maybe two and a half Long Island Teas – after that I'd be completely wasted."

It was a different world, and a language I didn't fully recognise, but Aitch was doing a good job of depicting his life partying hard in L.A. "My routine on Saturday nights," he continued, "was to eat dinner first, then to go drinking at one of my favourite bars and end up dancing all night long at my favourite club called Catch One. It was a massive warehouse on the wrong side of town, filled wall to wall with the most gorgeous men, and with two massive bars that each had at least a dozen men draped over them. There was also a VIP area on another floor but for once I avoided that, as my intent was always to hit the dance floor. I wanted to drink and to flirt. There was this amazing surround system and great music and I danced and danced and drank and drank until I was ready and hot.

Then around four o' clock in the morning, I'd usually find myself eating a Mexican burger with a coca cola, or going to the Jewish deli on Melrose and Switzer for pancakes. This was serious chill-out time, having worked really really hard during the week. And after all that, Jill," he said. "I'd still get up and go to church on Sunday morning."

I was so wrapped up in Aitch's story that I'd hardly noticed that my haircut was almost done. I still had a lot of questions about Aitch's time in L.A. and why he'd eventually given it all up, but by now Aitch was showing me the back of my hair in the small mirror, and it would soon be time to go. I reluctantly said my goodbyes and walked out of the salon. I was going to enjoy telling Mike about my haircut when I got home from work later in the day. He was used to my routine and rather predictable stories from the office, but tonight I'd got a much more interesting story to tell him.

If you really wish to be civilised you must be a snob throughout your life. You must learn to desire and enjoy the best. The best of everything is only just good enough.

Villiers David,
       Advice to my Godchildren

MY SWEET SUGAR MANDY

At my next appointment at the salon, Aitch greeted me as usual with his charming smile and a glance that seemed to say, 'Just you wait until you hear what I have to tell you about today'. I'd sat in the reception area trying to concentrate on reading *The Times*. But I was in a state of nervous excitement. I liked to think I was experienced; I'd met some extraordinary people in my time but I'd never met anyone quite like Aitch. I didn't know what I was going to find out next about him, but I sensed it might surprise or even shock me.

Once my hair had been washed and I was sitting comfortably in front of the mirror, we picked up our conversation again. I'd expected to hear more about his time in Los Angeles, but Aitch had obviously been thinking about his earlier life since he last saw me. As he took my hair between his fingers, he started to tell me a story – the story of a relationship he'd had with a guy called Ben in the 1970s.

"I can still remember the boxed mahogany toilet in his fancy Chelsea apartment," he was saying, in his typically mischievous way. "It was magnificent, and I'd never seen anything like it. Ben lived in some style with all sorts of beautiful 'objets'; it was hard for me to take it all in at first. In his sitting room there was a fabulous cabinet shaped like a pyramid full of antique silver salt and pepper pots. It was set between two ivory brocade sofas that were covered in silk embroidered cushions, and in the centre of the room there was an enormous coffee table with a Hermès ashtray in pride of place."

I had grown to love the way Aitch described things with such a luxury of detail. He was telling me about the first time he'd been to Ben's apartment in Cadogan Gardens. The interior had been designed by Robin Anderson, a well-known designer, socialite and friend of Ben's, and was clearly, from Aitch's description, a feast to the eye.

"It was the penthouse of course," he went on, "small and intimate, with oil paintings on the walls, and photographs of family and friends in silver frames on every surface. In his bedroom he had a rather grand four-poster bed, and in the dining room there was an antique table beautifully polished and adorned with silver initialled napkin rings and exquisite cut glass. Outside there was a roof terrace with a table and chairs and a stylish green parasol to sit under – the whole apartment screamed luxury, but not in an ostentatious way; everything was just so, in perfect placement, you might say."

I was starting to get the impression that this was quite a special relationship for Aitch, and I was curious to know more about it.

"How did you meet Ben?" I asked.

"It all started when I was working as a shampooist in a small salon called Robert Fielding's, opposite Mrs Beeton's bakery on the Kings Road in Chelsea", he said. "I was well received there and my boss Alan Hemmings and his wife Bonnie took me under their wing and looked after me. The clients at the salon were the Chelsea set, the sort of ladies who had their hair done every Friday before they went down to their country houses for the weekend. There were Hermès scarves everywhere," he laughed, "and a lot of Gucci."

"These clients were very particular," Aitch continued. "They had an assurance about how they wanted to look, and they conveyed confidence both in the way they spoke and how they moved. I learnt a lot about being attentive, listening to clients who were so much worldlier than I was, and asking discrete questions when appropriate.

"You have to understand this was a completely different world for me, Jill. I was living at home with my mum at the time. I reckon I took more taxis from Harlesden to Sloane Square than anyone else ever has," he giggled. "I felt a bit like an observer back then, taking it all in, and learning how to deal with clients. I was thrust into a situation where I found myself working with people from all over the world, from Australia to South Africa, and mixing with clientele from the upper classes."

I sat back in the chair and pictured Aitch as he carefully absorbed the ways of the Chelsea set, and started to use what he'd experienced to create an early version of his colourful trademark style. He'd learnt to spot an expensive handbag or scarf from two hundred yards, and he knew instinctively what each designer brand said about its owner. I dreaded to think what impression he'd formed of me – I'd always considered handbags a functional piece of my wardrobe rather than an indication of my style credentials.

"But how did you meet Ben?" I persisted. There was so much I still didn't know, and much more I wanted to understand. I silently willed Aitch to cut my hair more slowly to make sure I didn't miss out on any part of his stories.

"Well," he said, in a slightly conspiratorial tone. "One day I was browsing in a boutique called Just Men on the Kings Road. I didn't have the kind of money you needed to shop there myself of course, but I liked to look, and on that particular day I was running an errand for one of the stylists from Robert Fielding's. I was wearing my favourite tight-fitting hipsters with flared bottoms and a belt with a huge shiny buckle. I remember the flowered fitted shirt I was wearing, and how I loved the way it showed off my physique underneath with my dog tag necklace against my chest. I had a lot of swagger back then," Aitch said, "and I used to turn a lot of heads with my big Afro hair and my oxblood red platform shoes as I strolled down the Kings Road in the sunshine. If you look good you feel good," he said. "I learnt that from Vidal very early on, and since then I've always enjoyed making a statement by how I look and dress."

"So that's when you met Ben?" I asked.

"Well no actually," said Aitch, "but Ben was there and was watching me without me realising it."

"Go on," I said, intrigued by the scene of passive observation.

"A little while later," Aitch said, with a hint of mystery in his voice, "I was approached in the street by a guy I later knew to be Emile who said, 'A friend of mine would like to meet you.'"

"My god," I said, "weren't you taken aback and nervous about that?"

"Not at all," said Aitch, "I felt excited – in fact, I couldn't wait to meet this friend of his who I was told was called Ben. It was all very relaxed. I discovered later on that because Ben had spotted me in Just Men, he'd assumed I worked there or at least in one of the other shops nearby. He told me he'd searched high and low and ended up buying a whole new collection of socks while looking for me in all the menswear shops he could find on the Kings Road," Aitch laughed modestly at the recollection. "Finally when his sock drawer was full, Ben paid Emile to track me down and he found me walking home from Robert Fielding's one Saturday afternoon – apparently I wasn't that hard to spot!"

Just at that moment, another stylist called Aitch across the salon floor to consult with a client. I sat back in the chair and looked at myself in the mirror. My haircut was starting to take shape but I was preoccupied. What was I going to discover this time as his story unfolded?

Aitch returned smiling as broadly as ever, and apologetic for leaving me momentarily unattended. I knew that he wanted to tell me what had happened next just as much as I wanted to hear about it.

"In fact, I met Ben for the first time at the El Sombrero club," he said. "It was one of the early gay clubs in London and I'd never been there before. Emile took me there and introduced me to this dashing blond called Ben. I liked him instantly," said Aitch, "he made me smile; he had charisma and charm, with a confidence that came from his privileged upbringing. I can still remember what he was wearing the first time we met. He was impeccably dressed for the evening, with a Turnbull & Asser shirt, a peach cashmere sweater, a huge Cartier watch and Gucci shoes."

"We had to queue to get into the club," said Aitch, "but there was an instant connection between us. Once we went inside, the club was surprisingly small, but it was very cosy. It had warm lighting, and the décor was full of orange and ochre and deep red colours. It was amazing," said Aitch. "We were ushered to a table close to the dance floor, and I realised it had been reserved for us. It was actually the first time in my life, Jill, that I'd sat at a reserved table, and it felt very special being there with Ben. There was a bar at the back of the club where the serious drinkers hung out, but we were in the best seats in the house. A waiter came up to serve us and asked me what I was drinking. Quick as a flash I said 'champagne of course'", Aitch laughed; the lessons in the Chelsea lifestyle were already paying off.

"The Sombrero club was very relaxed," said Aitch, "it had an easy acceptance and wasn't hard-core or full of guys in leather. In those days that look didn't really appeal to me," he grinned. "My interest in leather came much later on, and I've never looked back!"

I hesitated too long to pursue this provocative statement before Aitch continued with his story. "I danced all night while Ben watched, mesmerised by me," said Aitch, "and although the club was full of people, it felt as if we had the place to ourselves. At the end of the evening Ben asked me politely if I'd like to go back to his place for coffee," he said, looking at me in the mirror with a distinct twinkle in his eye. "It was an invitation, but I didn't feel patronised or obliged," Aitch said. "He treated me with respect and I loved his obvious sophistication. He told me to wait outside the club while he went to get his car."

"As I stood there on the pavement, I couldn't believe my eyes when a gold Rolls Royce glided quietly up to the kerb and Ben opened the passenger door for me to get in. The car had a wickedly sexy dashboard and smelt of leather, and I felt really excited as we drove off to Sloane Square." There was a slight pause and then Aitch looked at me and grinned. "So that, Jill," he said triumphantly, "was how I met my sugar daddy."

It was an old-fashioned expression, but we both knew it was a relationship that was difficult to sum up in any other way. For my part, I'd never met anyone who'd had a sugar daddy before. It was thrilling, but it also felt a little dangerous. *What more would I discover,* I wondered, *and would it shock me?* I could tell that it was really important for me to understand this chapter in Aitch's life. It was part of his formation, a meaningful relationship that had shaped his character, and to some extent his future. He was young when he first met Ben, and he was exploring and experiencing new things in a world beyond his dreams.

"Ben taught me so much," said Aitch. "He used to recite passages of a book to me called *Advice to my Godchildren* by a guy called Villiers David. I've never read the book myself but it was sort of Ben's philosophy on life, and some of the phrases from the book stick with me even today. It was all about learning good manners and becoming a gentleman by appreciating the finer things in life. And it was about life as an adventure, exploring, absorbing and enjoying everything it had to offer."

"But my education was just as much about the experiences Ben introduced me to as what he said or quoted to me," Aitch continued. "We used to go down to the country at weekends for play-time with Ben's City gent friends. I remember driving down in his Rolls Royce to a big country house near Newbury one time. We swept up a long drive through manicured lawns and past the stables to a magnificent country house. It had a lake with a wide crescent of water at its entrance, and a river running underneath that you could see through a glass bottomed floor in the wine cellar. The house was full of beams with low ceilings and panelled walls in the bedrooms, with beautifully starched white linen on the beds. It was idyllic. Just being there, Jill, made me feel instantly happy. Ben and I would go horse riding in the early morning and come back to kedgeree for breakfast served by a butler. During the day we would play backgammon and drink wine. Ben's friends all had the best addresses of course – Ebury Street, Eaton Terrace, Glebe Place or anything ending in Mansions," he giggled. "It was certainly a long way from Manor Park Road in Harlesden where I was living with my mum."

A young assistant came over at that moment and spoke to Aitch. I watched as he patiently and discretely gave instructions. Always respectful, always attentive to others and ready to help and guide, just like he'd been taught as a young man all those years ago in the Kings Road. I noticed that he never barked instructions to the juniors like some of the other stylists. He'd never forgotten what he'd learnt from others and instinctively wanted to pass on his craft to others. As I client, I sensed the respect in which he was held by everyone in the salon. And my respect for him was growing too as I listened to his stories.

"It was my 21st birthday party not long after I met Ben," said Aitch.

We'd moved on to a new chapter in his story, and I sat back and listened. "It was the first party I'd had since my first communion as a small child, and if I'm honest, I felt cheated that I hadn't had another party since then. Looking back now I can see that it was very difficult for my mum. I was still living with her in Manor Park Road with my brother and my sisters. My mum was very reserved and it wouldn't have been easy for her to agree to a party for all my friends. I guess she must have been aware of my sexuality by then, but it was at that party that she saw it for the first time in her own home.

One of my friends called Larry turned up in a white jump suit, he looked camp and not a little ridiculous," he laughed, "but by this stage, I was completely enamoured with Ben and I was very excited about him coming to my party.

"By Ben's standards it was a pretty unsophisticated affair," Aitch said, "with finger sandwiches, hard-boiled eggs and cheese and onion crisps, but he liked me enough that he wanted to meet my family. It was a sign of his respect for me that he was prepared to turn up at a black family's home in Harlesden, a world away from Chelsea."

"In those days," said Aitch, "there were no parking meters, so Ben parked his gold-coloured Rolls Royce right outside our house. That got the neighbour's net curtains twitching, I can tell you Jill. He was extremely attentive and respectful to my mother, charming the pants off her like he did with everyone he met. But I could tell she really liked him too. I can still picture her standing in the hallway alongside my Aunty Shirley, the two of them with bemused smiles on their faces, watching us all having fun. Ben had a way of smiling and talking at the same time – and of course he brought with him a bottle of the best champagne. My mum was completely bowled over. She'd never held a bottle of champagne before."

I sat back and considered the situation. *What a remarkable woman Aitch's mother must be*, I thought. It was hard to imagine how she'd been so understanding and accepting of the situation she found herself in back then. She would have wanted her son to be happy, but this experience called for more than just motherly love. And then it occurred to me – it was Ben who had made her comfortable, Ben who had acted in a way that had made her feel special, Ben who had created an experience she would never forget.

"My mother kept that champagne bottle and its cork for years afterwards," Aitch added quietly.

"So tell me more about Ben," I said. "What was he like?"

"He had an Etonian look about him," Aitch replied, "with a cut-glass English accent and a real joie de vivre. He was devilishly handsome with blond hair, fair skin and piercing blue eyes. He had a sense of mischievousness and a provocative laugh, a kind of chuckle that made everyone smile."

"Sounds a bit like you," I said – "apart from the fair skin and blushed complexion!"

"If I have an ounce of what Ben had, I'm really lucky," said Aitch wistfully, and with a seriousness I hadn't expected. It made me realise that part of him was still in love with the way Ben had made him feel.

There was a moment of silence while Aitch reflected on the past, and I digested what I'd heard. So this was where his striking self-confidence had begun. This was the starting point of the creation of 'Aitch'.

"Ben was the stamp and the blueprint of who I am," he said. "He formed my DNA. From the moment I met him my story was set out. I learnt so much from him. He was caring and compassionate, he had a level of concern for others, and he was very sensitive to how I felt."

Our eyes met in the mirror and I knew he was talking from the heart. For a short moment, it was as if time had stood still. Then Aitch beamed, "And I learnt from his playfulness, not to take myself too seriously," he said.

The spell was broken and my haircut was nearly finished. Aitch put some gel on his fingers and rubbed it through my hair. Then he put his right hand on my head and twisted it back and forth. My hair moved beautifully and fell into a perfect shape.

"It always looks so much better when you do it," I said, as I admired myself in the mirror.

"Well if it starts looking better when you do it, then I'm in real trouble," Aitch said, and we both laughed as I picked up my bag and reluctantly went back to work.

I see people as shapes, bone structures, as animated subjects for the scissors. If there was a personal influence, it was Bauhaus, but it all had to be done with a pair of hands. Being a visual art, hair is far more emotional.

Vidal Sassoon

SCULPTURE IN MOTION

I looked in the mirror and couldn't help but laugh at myself. *Who'd have thought it?* There I was with a white bandana around my forehead, and with what looked like three enormous solar panels strategically placed around my head. I'd always wondered what other women were doing under these contraptions. I remembered the old style helmet heaters that women used to sit under at the hairdressers. It was an iconic image of the 1950s and '60s. The technology had clearly advanced since those days but these latest machines were, I imagined, doing pretty much the same job. I was giggling quietly to myself, however, as I'd never have thought that one day it would be me sitting under one of them.

For over fifty years, I'd resisted any treatment to my hair apart from a traditional wash, cut and blow-dry. Many hair stylists had tried and failed to persuade me over the years to have more treatments, but I was proud of the fact that I'd never had a perm or a colour put in my hair. I guess I was a little scared of it if I'm really honest. I didn't have enough confidence to take that extra step towards a different look. It was Aitch who'd finally given me what it took to get there, and the bonus for me was that with a longer appointment I had more time to talk to him.

"I think we might add a little colour today," he'd said casually, as we talked about what my hair needed, and momentarily I'd frozen in the chair. I had visions of going home with bright red hair or, God forbid, becoming a blonde. Aitch, of course, knew me well enough to gauge my reaction. "Just a natural wash," he said, "no chemicals, and with a chestnut colour that will enhance the natural tones in your hair – like newly formed conkers full of shine."

Aitch had this knack of making it sound quite wonderful. I loved the way he described the colour, and I felt as ready as I knew I ever would be to try it out. So it was off to have a second wash, and then to sit under this contraption and look at my ridiculous image in the mirror.

When Aitch returned, he unwound the bandana from my head and ran his fingers through my hair. The treatment hadn't been too bad an experience after all, but I was anxious to see how different my hair would look once it was dry. I didn't want to go back to work looking anything other than my normal professional self. Conscious of my anxiety, Aitch said quietly and reassuringly, "Please don't worry Jill, the colour is perfectly natural and will wash out of your hair in due course." I breathed more easily and sat back in the chair.

As Aitch started to work on my hair, I decided to ask him about his early training and his experiences of working with models. I was keen to understand how he'd learnt his craft. I'd read about the academy in Davies Mews that Vidal had set up, and knew that it was considered *the* place to go for young stylists. I also knew that Aitch had been a student there.

"It was the best training I could have asked for," Aitch said. "I'd had experience at Robert Fielding's of course, where I got the very basic training in setting, pinning curls and using tongs. That earned me a place at the academy, and it was there that I passed my cutting test and perfected my skills. It was pretty intensive training. There were certain iconic Sassoon haircuts that you had to learn – Firefly, Halo, Mouche and the Fall, for example." I pulled a face as Aitch reeled off the names. Given my lack of interest in hairdressing it was hardly surprising that I'd never heard of any of them before, and it amused me to think of haircuts having names all of their own.

"What happened after your initial training?" I asked.

"Well once I left the academy," said Aitch, "I went to work at the salon in Sloane Street. It was there that I started to develop my own techniques and styles, and was able to adapt the skills I'd learnt to the latest fashions and to become more creative. It was also there that I started to do photo sessions as well as working with my own clients at the salon."

I was impatient to know more about this, but it was clear that Aitch wanted me to understand first of all how he'd built on his training at the academy.

"As a stylist, you have to learn the basics really well first," he continued, "and you also need some natural flair and the ability to visualise a whole new look. You must be able to create an individual style for each client."

I had to admit I was quickly learning that there was a lot more to hair styling than I'd ever imagined. If I'm honest, I'd always assumed it was a fairly frivolous way of earning a living, and I'd no idea how much craft and technique were involved.

"How do you go about doing that?" I asked innocently.

"Well," said Aitch, "I start by looking at the whole person, how tall they are, the shape of their face, the style in which they dress, and who their favourite designers are. You learn to read what clients want by what they show you with their hands, and of course you learn to listen really carefully to them. I pay just as much attention to my clients' body language as to what they say, and then I assess what they've given to me in terms of ideas and inspiration. From all of that, I can envisage a look that will work really well for them. But it's not always easy to convey that to a client."

"What makes you say that?" I asked, wondering what Aitch's vision for me had been, and whether I'd made it easy or difficult for him to work towards it.

"Well this is where trust comes in", he said. "A client needs the confidence that you will do his or her hair well; entrusting your look to someone else can be quite intimidating. So you have to build that trust and confidence over time. I don't usually share the final vision

I have for each of my clients until I feel they are ready for it. Besides developing an individual style is usually something that evolves over time, with each haircut moving a step closer to the final look I have in mind for them."

Now I could see exactly how Aitch had been working with my own hair. When we'd first met he hadn't suggested a new style but just tightened the existing cut. Then gradually he'd been pushing the boundaries a little further at each session. He knew that right now I needed a look that reflected my professional position, but I could tell that he was able to envisage a time when that might change, and that he had a look in mind for me when that moment arrived.

"Clients can be quite unpredictable at times," Aitch continued.

"In what way?" I asked, hoping that he wasn't thinking of me.

"Well, sometimes they claim they want a change, but they aren't really prepared to move in a different direction. And there's often a boyfriend or a girlfriend in the background giving them views and opinions that may not be totally honest. Clients need to be prepared for a change and capable of living with those changes. My philosophy has always been that you should never give someone a haircut they can't carry off."

As Aitch explained it to me it was all very clear, obvious really, but not something I'd ever thought about before. There really was quite a lot of psychology at play in the whole relationship between stylist and client, and this was something that Aitch instinctively understood.

"You need to be able to give confidence to your client that you will do their hair well – and that's especially true on big occasions like weddings," Aitch said. "It's all about making the bride comfortable. At the early consultations you need to ask lots of questions – what's the back of the dress going to be like? Is there a tiara or headdress? Can the bride step into the dress or does it go over her head? – It's the small details that make a big difference to how you style the hair. And it's usually an on-going story, you have to expect some of the details to change, and you need to be able to put the bride at ease. I usually insist on a trial run before the big day. I arrive with my combs, my clips, and my assistants – and a lot of patience. You need to be organised to make the trial run as relaxed as possible, and you should expect the bride's hair not to do what it's supposed to do," Aitch laughed, and I smiled back at him in the mirror.

"Actually it's best not to linger overly long at that stage", he continued. "You have to take charge and not confuse your client with too many options. I use my experience and ability to visualise the final finish. Not all brides can do that for themselves, and that's why it's so important that you gain their trust."

"I guess a wedding can be quite hard work," I said, as I started to think about what was involved. "The morning of the wedding is a really nice time," said Aitch, "as you know you're going to spend the day making the bride look radiant. And while of course I don't insist on it," he giggled, "it's always lovely to start with a champagne breakfast with fresh fruits and croissants. There's a distinct sexiness about a good breakfast, for sure." Aitch paused and I thought about my own breakfast that morning – a couple of Weetabix clearly wasn't what Aitch had in mind.

"I also believe that personal presentation as a stylist is really important," he continued. "I nearly always wear a suit for example. I like to look my best even though in reality I spend a lot of my time under the bride's skirts pulling down this and that – it's not all glamorous."

Aitch giggled again and so did I. I could just imagine him with his head under a huge petticoat and his long legs sticking out underneath – adorned, of course, in the latest designer shoes.

Then I noticed a kind of mistiness come over him. "All brides change on the day of their wedding," Aitch sighed, "they become serene with an almost ethereal quality about them, and it can get quite emotional. You see the parents' pride in their daughter, and you know their teary eyes represent sheer happiness. It's a real privilege to be part of that." Aitch was genuinely moved and I could tell how much he threw himself into making every bride's day really special. At that moment, I wished he'd been at my own wedding to have done the same for me.

"Of course, I did a lot special events in L.A.," Aitch said, breaking out of his own reverie. "Opulent private parties in mansions, on yachts and once an outrageous party on a train where everyone was taking cocaine. But I loved doing beautiful weddings on the manicured lawns of the Beverly Hills Hotel most of all. There would be an army of fit young waiters in immaculately tailored uniforms wandering around serving everyone champagne and the most exquisite canapés – quite divine. I remember on one occasion the reception was actually held on the roof of the hotel. The bride was a carefree kind of a girl. She worked as a personal stylist at one of the top boutiques in Rodeo Drive, so there were a lot of celebrities there as guests as well as people from the fashion world. The reception was held under the stars and there was humidity in the air as she swirled around the dance floor. A lot of the time you don't see brides really enjoying themselves on their wedding day, but this bride looked radiantly happy all night long. That's the type of wedding I really enjoy."

"Another time," he giggled, as he summoned up memories from the hundreds of weddings he'd obviously been to, "my partner Donald and I ended up in the limo with the bride! The wedding was actually taking place in one of the pods on the London Eye. I attended to the bride and as we helped to lift her dress into the car, she looked at us and pleaded with us rather sweetly 'please come with me'. I'm thinking this doesn't seem right," said Aitch, "but she insisted, and so we turned up with her, one on each arm, much to the surprise of the rest of the wedding guests. I still do her hair regularly in the salon and she often reminds me of that special day.

I realise now that it was a sign of respect, a kind of respect that money can't buy."

I knew from our previous conversations that Aitch had worked with many famous photographers, and that he'd done beauty shots for magazines as well as editorial shots. This seemed like the ideal moment to move the conversation on. "Tell me about your work in the studio," I said.

"Well Jill," he said, "I started assisting on photo sessions to begin with, working with Pat Lewis. She was the assistant to Henry Abell when he was art director at the Sloane Street salon, and she was a real master of editorial hair sessions. Pat's work was highly influential in her day, groundbreaking you could say – it was a romantic look and she created an ethereal finesse to the finish of each editorial creation. I found it quite beautiful and was captivated by her work. I was inspired by her and emulated her style while adding my own personal twist to it. That's really important in a hairstyling career – to be inspired by others, or by what you see around you, to develop your style from that, and over time to establish your own signature or brand."

As Aitch explained it to me, it was obvious but it made me think. I could see the parallels with professionals in other less obviously creative fields who built their personal brand or reputation by learning from their mentors and through their experiences.

"Beauty shots are taken in a studio," Aitch continued, "and the photographs are taken really close up to the model. So the hair has to be sharp and cleanly presented. As a stylist you need to have a very good relationship with the make-up artist, as it's crucial that the make-up and hair work well together in the photograph. It's also critical that you have a rapport with the model. You need to be able to judge her reaction to the experience, and create the right sort of confidence in her pose. It was all high camp at the time," said Aitch breaking out into a laugh, "and we had great fun mimicking their poses and giving them silly names."

He paused and struck a pose for me in the mirror with a pinched face and arms wrapped around his body. "Just like this," he said, and I couldn't help but laugh.

"Very early on in my career I had my biggest break," Aitch continued once he'd stopped laughing. "I was asked to do a fashion shoot for Italian *Vogue* with David Bailey. It was my very first shoot, and as anyone in the business will tell you Jill, it doesn't get much better than that. Six full pages in one of the most well regarded fashion magazines, working with David Bailey at the height of his fame. I was really really excited about the megawatt profile that came with it, and it was amazing to think that it had all come about because Pat Lewis was unavailable and had recommended me for the job. I didn't fully appreciate the importance of getting credits at first," Aitch continued, "but I quickly learnt that 'Hair by Aitch Peters' made a real difference to my professional reputation, especially when it appeared in leading magazines such as *Vogue*, *Harpers & Queen* and *Cosmopolitan*."

"What was it like working with David Bailey?" I asked, "Especially as you were so young – weren't you terrified?"

"I can still remember it like it was yesterday," said Aitch, looking a little wistful. "It was a miserable rainy day and I had to go straight from the Sloane Street salon to Bailey's home in Hampstead where he had his studio. I was really nervous as you might imagine, and I ended up getting lost and arriving dreadfully late. It didn't help my nerves that when I eventually got there, Bailey was absolutely furious and screamed and swore at me. In fact, there was a lot of profanity that I wasn't used to. The models used the F-word in a way I wasn't expecting, and compared with how I'd been brought up, there seemed to me to be a complete lack of manners in how people behaved. I guess I was quite naïve, but I'd imagined that the models would be all prim and poised. The whole experience momentarily deflated my self-confidence, to be honest with you, but I quickly realised I needed to get over it. I can remember thinking, *'Okay, if this is how it's going to be I need to learn, and I need to learn fast.'*

"In my early days, I also went along to style hair at the degree shows at St Martin's College of Art," Aitch continued, "and from there I started to build a reputation for myself as well as widening my network of designers, models and photographers. For fashion shows you needed to be good, but you also had to have a certain speed about you, and you had to be liked by the makeup artists, models and photographers in the team. The model might only be on the catwalk for seven or nine minutes, but there'd be several changes of clothes and hair during that time. You had to have done your homework to know what outfits and hats were going to be used and in what order."

"I also got to work on editorial shoots, which are quite another thing altogether," Aitch said. "They're shot more at a distance and you have to allow the image to tell its own story. As a hair stylist, one of your roles is to contribute to the mood of the shot by encouraging the model to strike a particular pose, and to praise her when she looks good. Then everyone in the team gets in a huddle with the Polaroids to check that the lighting and every detail is right before the final shots are taken."

Aitch paused and looked at me in the mirror. "It was experiences like these Jill," he said, "that taught me the importance of performance. Once the models were under the lights on the catwalk they were literally transformed into completely different beings – from foul-mouthed young girls to the epitome of pure elegance."

It was an interesting statement that I reflected on as Aitch excused himself and went across to the reception desk to check up on his next appointment. I sat back in the chair for a moment and closed my eyes. I was struck by how so much of what Aitch had learnt about the importance of performance and presentation, in addition to the technical elements of his craft, had great similarity with my experience in the business world. Being technically competent was only ever half the story. Success was so much more down to the psychology of interacting with others, and building trust and relationships.

"It's always fascinating working with models," said Aitch on his return. I spent a lot of time observing how they twisted their bodies, using their elbows to create a distinctive shape. They're statuesque creatures who elongate their frames to hold a particular pose. My first experience of doing the hair for a couture collection was at the House of Dior, would you believe, in Conduit Street – what's now the Sketch club, where all the A-listers go.

"Back then, to enter the House of Dior was the ultimate experience in sophistication, and a lesson for me in the world of sheer couture. I walked inside, feeling the luxuriousness of the goose grey carpets under my feet, and pausing to admire two of the biggest arrangements of white lilies I'd ever seen. I could feel a sense of sublime luxury in the room. There were fabulous taffeta curtains adorning the entrance to the catwalk, and which looked to me like giant bird wings. Tiny gilded chairs with crimson velvet cushions added to the grandeur of the scene, and the whole room smelt divinely of Dior's signature fragrance 'Diorella'.

"I stood there transfixed for a few moments, absorbing the atmosphere through all my senses. Then just as I was coming to terms with the prestige of the occasion, one of the staff whispered in my ear that Princess Margaret would be attending the show as he carefully placed an ashtray next to her designated chair. That was a first for me, Jill – being in the same room as a member of the Royal family."

"What was the show itself like?" I asked.

"Being naturally curious, I peeped through the taffeta curtains as the show started," Aitch replied. "I wanted to see the girls perform. It was a show of pure elegance – in total contrast to how the models had appeared when they first arrived. They looked plain and ordinary to me, even a bit wrecked in some cases. But here they were doing what they did best; all made up with beautiful hair and dressed in exquisite couture gowns. They were quite extraordinary, and so was their transformation into the most gorgeous creatures as soon as they stepped into the limelight. I was mesmerised as I watched them saunter down the catwalk with their exceptionally long legs and complete command of the audience. They would fix their gaze at eye level in a delayed poise as they reached their final pose – and some of them had a whole repertoire of really wicked looks. Each model had a kind of assurance in her stride, like a thoroughbred, yet at the same time they glided down the catwalk like gazelles."

I reflected on the artifice that went into creating glamour, and as Aitch paused for breath I thought of him surrounded by models and the frenzy of the catwalk show – taking it all in and quietly learning his trade. After a few moments he continued.

"My fascination with posture was what led to my interest in ballet," he said. "I'd learnt about its importance from the Alexander Technique classes I'd attended, and I was interested in the role posture played in good physique. I first started going to the ballet with a friend of mine who was half-Norwegian. We used to go regularly to the Coliseum and I remember seeing Rudolf Nureyev and Margot Fonteyn perform there in *Swan Lake* – God that takes me back."

"Wow, that must have been an amazing experience," I said.

"Actually at the time," Aitch replied, "there was a lot of snobbery about going to the ballet. It implied a certain lifestyle, if you understand me, but thankfully I was so naïve at the time I was oblivious to what some people were no doubt thinking about me being there – in tow as it were. In those days, I enjoyed the intermission as much as the performance to be honest with you, as I loved watching everyone in their finery. I would stand spellbound in the bar observing every detail of how these ballet lovers, who to me were so stylish, handled themselves with sophisticated assurance."

"Later on, when I was with Ben, he and I went to see the Alvin Ailey dance company which included the first black male ensemble. Given that he loved young black men, it was just perfect for him; he had a real thing about black dancers on points at one stage," Aitch laughed, "so much so that he threw a party for the whole cast at this flat in Glebe Place just off the Kings Road. I was intimidated, totally totally intimidated by the occasion, but I was also excited to be up close and personal with the dancers," he gushed.

"Sadly I ended up rather disappointed as the dancers didn't have any of the wow factor I was expecting when I first met them. They were really quite casual out of character, and didn't make any special effort to be graceful off the stage. At the time, recreational pleasures – if you get my meaning – were also the order of the day and I have to tell you the dancers fully embraced them."

I wasn't sure I did understand exactly what Aitch was implying and my expression in the mirror gave my uncertainty away.

"Purple hearts and brown candy were pretty common at the time," Aitch explained, "although I wasn't part of that scene myself. In fact," he laughed, "I sometimes think I missed out on the whole purple heart thing because when I got back to London from L.A., they were already out of fashion – by then everyone was taking ecstasy."

"It became clear to me," Aitch continued, before I had a chance to quiz him about his experiences with drugs, "that dancers were very different creatures from models. They have a completely different sense of awareness. Models are always conscious of how they sit – they want to make an elegant shape or a statement with their bodies. Dancers however, in my experience, take up awkward, almost unattractive positions, when they finish their performance."

Aitch stopped cutting and put his hands on my shoulders as if to make a statement. "I have to tell you Jill," he said, "I found the women dancers particularly unsexy, especially when compared with the models I worked with. The male dancers are much more attractive as far as I'm concerned. They show a lot of muscle extension, tautness and rigidity and I've always found that attractive. Their physicality and their well-toned chests; it's all very very sensual, and gives them a god-like quality in my eyes – to be worshipped you might say."

I swallowed hard and looked at Aitch in the mirror. For a moment, I wasn't sure where the conversation was going to next. I was a little nervous about how I would react to more details about Aitch's sexual attractions, but I needn't have worried. He knew the limits of my sensibilities, and perhaps conscious of the salon setting, he picked up the conversation again by resuming his thoughts about the ballet.

"Those early experiences with Ben were the start of my lifelong fascination with ballet dancing and dancers, Jill," he said. "I've seen performances all over the world, in San Francisco and L.A., and once I even went to see the Cuban dance company in Havana; Carlos Acosta was the leading dancer and choreographer at the time, and the company had an amazing combination of elegance and pace that I've never seen before or since."

"Which are your favourites out of all the ballets you've seen?" I asked.

Aitch thought for a moment before replying. It was obvious this wasn't an easy question for him to answer. "Well my favourite ballets have got to be the classics of *Swan Lake* and *Sleeping Beauty,*" he said, "but I also love some of the modern stuff from the more avant-garde companies, and I adore anything by Kenneth Macmillan – he's my all-time favourite director. Then, of course, I can't resist the Russian dancers from the Kirov or the Bolshoi – my heart simply misses a beat when I watch them dance. I loved the recent production of *Eugene Onegin* choreographed by Boris Eifman, and having seen the film, and the ballet of *Anna Karenina*, I've completely fallen in love with Russian drama."

I waited while Aitch searched for the right hairbrush in his leather bag. I'd never met anyone who'd seen Nureyev and Fonteyn dance together, or anyone who'd seen such an eclectic range of ballets. I'd started to think about things I'd never really thought about before; the parallels between the technical craft of hairdressing, modelling and dance were a revelation to me.

"Poise is really important as a hair stylist," Aitch continued, "and the funny thing is I've often been mistaken for a dancer. In fact, Debbie Allen thought I was a dancer when she first met me – and, you know Jill, I actually feel like a leading dancer at times when I arrive at the salon, especially just after I've been to see a performance of the ballet. I take on the role of the leading man in a kind of out-of-body experience," he said, with a deep laugh, and I made a mental note to see if I could spot him doing that one time. No matter whether he'd just been to the ballet Aitch had a distinctive way of walking, pushing his hips forward and gliding effortlessly across the room.

"You do have a very distinctive walk," I said, keen for him to know that I'd noticed.

"It comes from my fear of old age, Jill," he replied smiling at me. "I'm determined to keep a young stride and stance, to walk with my signature confidence. I believe in keeping my body in good shape; you need to have a strong core as a stylist as the movements you make put enormous pressure on your back; and you need to be flexible and supple to manoeuvre around the chairs in the salon all day – of course, I also need to keep up with all the fit young guys around here," he laughed, in a way I knew meant he was deadly serious.

I found myself looking around the salon at the other stylists out of the corner of my eye, to see how they stood and held themselves. There were three or four young stylists working with clients around the salon. They were all clearly professional, but it struck me that none of them had yet developed the distinctive presence that Aitch brought to the room.

"So do you go to the gym regularly?" I asked.

"Yes, I've always worked out," Aitch replied, "to develop my upper body – that's what clients see in the mirror every day. I know it's really important to keep up my fitness, but sometimes I struggle to maintain my optimum level. I have to remind myself that my body also needs to get natural rest – you have to listen to your body and respond to it. When I was in L.A., I would go to the gym every morning and Paco my personal trainer would come round to my apartment to help me do my weights and teach me Tai Chi once a week.

"Nowadays, I like to have a work out each morning before I start in the salon," he said. "It makes me more acute in my work and gives me a fuller day. If you master your craft, your clients trust that you will deliver to that high standard every time they visit the salon. That means that every single haircut is important, however simple or however challenging it might be, and especially if it's the last appointment of the day. I like a powerful finish to my day, it makes me feel ready for the next day, and so I really challenge myself not to be complacent. It's something I learnt very early on in my career.

"During my training Chris Brooker, who was the creative director of Vidal Sassoon at the time, used to say to me 'you're only as good as your last haircut' and that's the key. If you're spirited into an appreciation of what you are doing, that comes across in your work and your clients come back again and again."

I smiled quietly to myself at what Aitch had said. The statement from Chris Brooker was a variation of a phrase I'd heard many times before in business: 'you're only as good as your last deal', the lawyers I worked with would regularly say.

"What else did Chris teach you?" I asked, curious to see if there were other parallels.

"Well Jill," Aitch replied, "Chris was always very professional, but he was also quite draconian. He had a thing about egos – he used to tell us all to leave our egos at the door of the salon. I used to watch how he held himself in the salon, just like the actor I'd always wanted to be, and it made me realise that in the salon I had my very own theatrical stage to perform on. I was never really sure whether Chris liked me, but I greatly admired him and his work.

"Later on in my career I shared a stage with him at the Royal Albert Hall and at Wembley arena and we did some fabulous demonstrations together. That was at the time when working with extensions really started to get going and I created a haircut with a helter-skelter effect by weaving wigs and fabrics into the model's hair – I actually got a standing ovation for that haircut, and it made me very proud to stand there beside Chris to receive it.

"I've learnt such a lot over the years," Aitch said, "but my prime aim is always to see a secret smile from my clients at the end of each haircut – the one that says I look good and I feel good."

It was time to go and as I left the salon with my deep chestnut hair shining in the daylight, I was deep in thought. I'd learnt a lot from this conversation with Aitch. It was clear to me now that a successful hair stylist needed the technical skills of a master craftsman, the physical strength of a performer and the instinctive sensitivity of an artist. It was a peculiarly demanding profession. His words about that secret smile were ringing in my ears. As I glanced at my reflection in the salon window, I knew exactly what he meant.

Be high-spirited, self-confident,
impertinent, if you will; even be outrageous,
but never be conceited.

Villiers David,
      Advice to my Godchildren

CITY OF ANGELS?

All of a sudden my appointments at the hairdressers had become non-negotiable, even if an important meeting came up. I briefed my personal assistant to this effect, and she looked at me somewhat askance. I knew what she was thinking: this is so unlike Jill, what's come over her? But despite my keenness to listen to more of Aitch's stories, and to understand his life story in more detail, I still found it hard to get to the salon on the prescribed six-week cycle. So by the time I arrived eight weeks or so later, I was full of anticipation – and in urgent need of a haircut.

Aitch was giggling as we picked up the conversation. He had a charming boyish playfulness about him, especially when he was about to reveal something he knew would surprise or amuse me.

"She just loved my swagger," he said, trying hard to suppress his own amusement. He was talking about Debbie Allen again; the American actress, choreographer and TV director who'd won an Emmy and a Golden Globe for her role as Lydia Grant in *Fame* in the early '80s.

"She used to come to the salon to have her nails done," he went on, "and after a while she asked me to work on her hair and make-up for the TV show she was directing and producing at the time called *A Different World*. I kept very close to her as I knew my constant attendance in the shadows gave her all the reassurance she needed during her preparation to direct the show. She knew I'd always make sure she looked good. As we got to know each other, she used to sing to me while I did her hair – mostly it was, *You've got the look*, which made us both laugh."

"How lovely," I said, wondering whether the song was a reference to Debbie Allen's own reflection in the mirror or, more likely, a comment about Aitch himself. I could see how he would make an impact in that milieu; he stood out from other people, with a distinctive style all of his own.

"It was through Debbie," said Aitch, "that I met Whoopi Goldberg for the first time. She was a good friend of Debbie's and I found her to be charming, witty and intelligent. She used to tease me by saying that my skin was just like dark chocolate mousse."

Well she was right about that, I thought, as I looked at Aitch in the mirror. He did have the most fantastic skin tone.

"Whoopi had a wonderfully comedic style," Aitch went on, "which I tried to reflect when I did her hair for her appearance on the Debbie Allen show. My inspiration actually came from a window display that I saw one day as I cruised along the streets of L.A. in my car. It was a wedding display full of the most beautiful white bridal bows. I developed the idea by placing enormous pewter-coloured bows in her hair that reflected the light right on to her dreadlocks. She absolutely loved it, and I have to say it did look pretty amazing."

"As I got more established in L.A.," Aitch said, "I was asked to clients' homes for private styling sessions – making house calls so to speak," he said smiling. "It was often at unsocial hours but I loved the intimacy of the experience. One of my favourite experiences was working with Tracy Ullman and her daughter. I went to her home three years running in preparation for The Emmys. In fact, Tracy pointed out to me that every year I did her hair she won an Emmy, and she had them all displayed on her mantelpiece to show me. That's probably why she kept inviting me back," Aitch said, smiling broadly – "nothing to do with the fabulous haircuts; I just became her lucky talisman!"

"What was it like moving to Los Angeles?" I asked, wanting to take him back to our previous conversation about developing his Californian lifestyle.

To my surprise, he replied in a serious tone. "To be honest it was a pretty stressful time for me at first. I had to find somewhere to live and at the same time I needed to establish myself as the new guy at the salon. I also had to take a practical cosmetology test when I arrived in the States to get a US stylist's license, even though I was the creative director – and to my great embarrassment, I failed it the first time around. That was a big worry for me and I felt anxious and alone. You see the test over there didn't just involve cutting hair – that was the easy bit – I also had to learn how to do eyebrow shaping, eyelash curling and how to put on false acrylic nails – and I had to learn fast."

I could feel Aitch's discomfort as he described his experience. It was easy to forget that when he'd first gone over to L.A., he was young and less experienced. He'd clearly been a fish out of water for a while.

"Very early on," said Aitch, his voice back to its normal confident tone, and as if wishing to move on quickly from a difficult memory, "I was invited over to Vidal's home. He'd bought it from Sylvester Stallone and it was the biggest mansion I'd ever seen. He asked me to come over there to cut his own hair and that of his family. I can still picture the scene," he said. "It was a very grand setting and the family were all sitting on sun-loungers around the pool. I didn't realise what was required at first, but then it dawned on me that they expected me to cut their hair al fresco as it were.

"I can tell you, Jill, that was another first for me," Aitch laughed, "but it was also a very personal experience, and I felt real warmth from Vidal and his family as I cut their hair away from the normal protocols of the salon. They dropped their guards a little, and so did I, but despite that there was still a lot of respect, and I appreciated that.

"Los Angeles was really very different from anything I'd experienced before," Aitch continued, "but I drew on all the experiences I'd had back in London, particularly the photographic sessions I'd been involved in. I'd learnt to understand the connection between the photographer and the fashion editor and the model, and what my role was in the whole affair. Sometimes there was a bit of conflict around, as you'd expect with so many egos in one room – you know who's the king or queen on the day," Aitch said, rolling his eyes, "but I learnt that with a bit of trust between us, we usually worked something out. There was a creative intensity in the way the photographers and editors worked, and I learnt to adopt that in my own consultations and on-going attendance to my clients.

"I feel privileged to have worked with some of the top fashion and beauty photographers – Lord Lichfield, Annie Liebovitz, Mario Testino, Lord Snowdon, Nick Knight, and Barry Lategan – and they all made a huge impact on me. I learnt from them how to listen to clients and to respect them, while at the same time having the presence and confidence to be in command of each creative situation."

It was interesting listening to Aitch dropping name-bombs all over the place. From anyone else it would have come across as showing off, but Aitch always told his stories with two parts chutzpah and one part self-effacement. He had a charming smile and a knowing look that disarmed any sense of hubris.

It was obvious that Aitch had loved every aspect of L.A. and made it his business to enjoy everything it had to offer.

"It was a place centred on looking and feeling good," he continued. "Everyone, and I mean everyone, had a weekly manicure and pedicure and regular massages – so I did the same. I also bought myself a special edition white VW convertible. It was Chris Brooker actually who persuaded me to buy it – he said it went with my image. Of course, it was always sunny in California and it gave me a real thrill to cruise around in my car with the top down on roads that stretched ahead for miles into the horizon. It was just like being in the movies." Aitch sighed, and put his hands on my shoulders for a moment. "I always thought there was something romantic, almost angelic, about my shiny white car, Jill," he said, "I would turn the music right up, and take great pleasure in overtaking all the black Cadillacs. I'd drive for hours, with my bare chest drenched in luxurious sun oils – always to a certain destination and of course always with intent."

It was an arresting image laced with innuendo and I wasn't sure whether Aitch wanted me to ask him more about that intent or not. Whatever his intention, he'd conveyed a feeling of sheer hedonism.

Somewhat to my surprise, Aitch switched from a frivolous to a darker tone of voice as he continued his story. "Not all the experiences I had in L.A., however, were good ones," he said. "Sometimes the situations I found myself in were edgy or downright dangerous, Jill. Being black, and driving a car like that I was regularly stopped by the Beverly Hills police asking for my details."

"Oh, how awful for you," I said, looking concerned, and wondering how hostile the police might have been with him.

"Actually I used to look forward to it," Aitch said grinning from ear to ear, and I realised he'd succeeded in teasing me again. "It gave me the opportunity to perve at their pristine uniforms and shiny high boots. The Beverly Hills police were a very handsome squad; in fact, they were quite the best presented police force I'd come across."

I glanced at Aitch in the mirror with a look that acknowledged his joke, and he winked back at me. "The police women were pretty fit too," he continued. "Being L.A., of course a lot of them had had breast surgery and with their bullet proof vests on they had, let's just say… very impressive carriages." I raised my eyebrows at his mischievous description. "For the record, Jill," he said, "I do find women sexy and attractive as well as men. Over the years I've had some of my most pleasurable encounters with the female sex – I like the power that emanates from the sort of women who go for it, who show a lot of confidence."

I wondered whether I was going to hear more about these pleasurable encounters, and whether Aitch was really as bisexual as he was implying, but he quickly returned to his story about life in L.A.

"There was also one very scary occasion when I was robbed at gunpoint," he said. "Two guys came up to me with guns in their hands and demanded everything I had. I was terrified but I just handed everything over to them – all I managed to hold onto was the photo of my mum that I had in my wallet." There was a pause as if Aitch was turning the experience over again in his mind. "But I have to say Jill, despite that, Los Angeles was really a most fantastic place to live. There were new restaurants opening every other week, wonderful bars, bakeries and coffee shops, and I loved people watching on Sunset Boulevard.

"Of course," he laughed, "the whole L.A. concept of valet parking was right up my street. I used to drive to work early in the morning and pull into the most beautiful parking lot – it was pristine and felt like parking in a museum. The valet would approach me in his smart uniform and white gloves and take my car keys before wishing me a nice day. I felt like a film star every time."

"Tell me about the salon in Beverly Hills," I said, imagining it to be the ultimate in chic pampering. Aitch smiled, and I detected a small sigh as he recalled the memory.

"For sure," he said. "The salon was in Rodeo Drive which is, of course, *the* premier street. It was lined with exotic flowers and so clean you could've eaten your dinner off the sidewalk. The entrance to the salon itself was magnificent with a grand marble staircase, which led up to the reception area, graced by the most beautifully presented girls. It was such a gorgeous place, very modern, but with décor unlike anywhere else. It made you feel good as soon as you came in. You walked past reception and along a corridor like a hall of mirrors – you could see your reflection everywhere, from floor to ceiling, and I used to love watching my clients preening and adjusting themselves as they walked from one treatment to another.

"At the back of the salon, there were banks of manicure stations where ladies would sit with their exposed toes shining in every shade of nail polish. Acrylic nails were all the rage at the time and you'd see clients fanning one hand furiously to dry their nails.

"We tried to think of absolutely everything in the salon," said Aitch. "So rather than clients having to root around in their handbags for their keys, and risking chipping their nail polish, we used to hang them up on a row of hooks like jailors keys. Then we'd present them back to them as they went to pick up their cars from the valet parking area."

I'd heard it all now. *What more would I discover about this salon?* I wondered.

"Just off the corridor of mirrors," Aitch continued on cue, "was the infamous VIP room."

"Infamous for what?" I asked.

For once Aitch looked a little embarrassed. "Well, it gained a certain reputation you understand, Jill. In those days, most of the staff were using coke... allegedly, of course," he added quickly, "... and apparently the room was sometimes used for naughty things."

It was a strange expression and I knew I couldn't leave it at that. "Naughty things?" I asked quizzically.

"Well it was a room that only the more senior staff members had a key to," said Aitch, "and the most exclusive, some might say debauched, parties used to take place there. It was all a bit like a glamorous version of the movie *Shampoo*," he added, "except more so."

Aitch moved away to find a hairbrush and left me to reflect on this revelation. I desperately tried to remember the plot of *Shampoo*, a film I'd seen many years ago, in the days when hairdressing really wasn't that interesting to me. There was certainly a lot of sexual indulgence in it as far as I could recall. Then the image came to me of Warren Beatty having vigorous sex on the kitchen floor and being interrupted by the woman's lover. Before I could start to work out what this implied about goings on in the VIP room, Aitch was back by my side telling his story.

"When I was there, it was quite different of course, Jill," he said. "Although I did once do Annie Lennox's hair in that VIP room."

I wasn't sure whether to believe that he'd not been involved in the sex and drugs scene at the salon, but now was not the time to probe him further about it. Instead Aitch continued his recollections about Annie Lennox, one of the heroines of my younger days.

"I remember how striking she was as she walked down that mirrored catwalk in the salon with no make-up," he said. "She just had a vivid flash of red lipstick, and of course, the most amazing blond haircut."

Aitch stopped cutting my hair and looked at me directly in the mirror. "For me, the Beverly Hills salon was just the very best," he said. "It had all the elements of a fully equipped spa, and the place oozed glamour from every pore. There was a beauty station with two beauticians making up clients all day long. They sat in sumptuous leather chairs looking up at the black and white photos of the creative team's latest collection. It was the '80s and the fashions were…well, as you might imagine, completely frivolous," he said, leaning forward and giving me one of his knowing looks.

"Don't forget, Jill," he went on, "I was the new boy from London. I had to impress the team with my ideas and my credentials to win respect as their creative director. From the start, I wanted to make the salon special. So I introduced client soirées when we would put on demonstrations of different haircuts using models dressed in lingerie. They were a great success and became quite a talking point in L.A."

I could well believe that, but I was intrigued. "Didn't other salons put on demonstrations then?" I asked.

"Yes Jill, they did", Aitch replied, "but demonstrations were typically only for the trade or for training purposes. I felt that our clients should also get a privileged glimpse into what we did, and how we did it. We would send out the most divine invitations to our regular clients on stiff white card with gold lettering and a request to RSVP. I made sure that everyone who came was welcomed with a glass of champagne and a choice of the best canapés, and we laid on dry ice and music to create a special atmosphere. It gave me great pleasure to see the look on my clients' faces as we showed off our latest collection."

Aitch was in his element and his memories were flooding back. "At Halloween one year we put on a really amazing show," he said. "I made a grand entrance into the salon dressed as Tina Turner with her song *What's Love Got To Do With It* blaring out through the loudspeakers. I'd made myself a fabulous wig and was wearing a short skirt and false fingernails to complete the look. I did have one problem though. I could only put the false nails on one hand as I needed to hold my scissors with the other one."

Aitch stepped back and held the pose for me behind my seat, grinning broadly as he did so. I sat back and laughed out loud. I didn't need any more prompting to picture Aitch in that get-up, prancing around in a raunchy show of camp bravado, with all eyes on him as he showcased his skills. He would have been in his element.

"I used to pick up ideas from all sorts of places," he went on. "For instance, I noticed that the best designer stores in Beverly Hills always had beautiful displays of flowers in their entrances, and they offered glasses of champagne and fresh fruit to their clients as they came in to shop. I quickly followed suit and introduced the same welcome to clients at the salon – flowers are always such a good thing, don't you think," he smiled.

"I got a lot of respect from my colleagues for the changes I introduced, and from the fact that celebrities were increasingly attracted to the salon. My first clients were actually the Thompson Twins," he said, "but others quickly followed through word of mouth. Our clients were often generous and we were regularly given tickets for concerts at places like the Hollywood Bowl. I liked to give the tickets to the juniors to thank them for their efforts.

"I worked with loads of big stars," continued Aitch. "Legends really – people like Mariah Carey, Jody Watley, Nicolas Cage, Jerry Hall and Emma Soames. Some of them like Saffron Burrows and Lorraine Pascale were young models in those days, and they've since gone on to become famous actresses and TV presenters in their own right."

It was obvious that Aitch had a real fondness for the people he'd met as he reflected on the memories. It had been a time of great excitement and glamour, but most of all he'd really enjoyed working with models and helping his clients, however famous they were, or were to become, to feel good and to look good. Most of us meet only one or two celebrities in our lifetimes, but Aitch had lived and worked amongst them, to the point that they were no longer celebrities to him, but real people that he knew and respected.

He was carefully trimming my fringe by this stage and was looking at me directly rather than through the mirror. I looked into his deep brown eyes and saw nostalgia for a time of great happiness in his life.

"L.A. was a real eye-opener for me," he went on, picking up on my curiosity to hear more. "I couldn't believe how seriously people took the party lifestyle, and how important it was to look good before going out on a Friday night. The women would all troop into the salon to have their hair and nails done, and I soon developed a routine all of my own. When I got home from the salon, the first thing I did was to ring up for a bottle of Veuve Clicquot. The deliveryman instantly recognised me from my English accent and would say 'Of course, Mr Peters,'" Aitch giggled.

"Then I'd have a shower and a shave and as I came out of the bathroom, I would hear the ding-dong of the doorbell and a bottle of chilled champagne would be carefully placed on my doorstep. There really is nothing nicer than having a cold glass of champagne as you get ready to go out," Aitch said, "and Veuve Clicquot quickly became my favourite. I would drink it very slowly as I dressed for the evening, and it would help to get me into the zone."

"The gay clubs in West Hollywood were amazing," Aitch continued, "and that's where I went most nights to dance until the early hours of the morning. I used to go to Catch One a lot. There was always a wall of gorgeous-looking black and Latino men to greet me when I went inside. It was at that club that a new adventure started when I managed to lose my passport there."

"Why did you have your passport with you?" I asked curiously.

"Well," Aitch explained, "you needed to show ID to get into any of these clubs, and as a foreigner that meant my passport. I'm still not quite sure how it happened, but one time after I'd been there I discovered when I got home that my passport had gone missing from my pocket. I was quite worried about it, and was busy making plans in my head about what I was going to tell my company, particularly about how and where I'd lost it. But from a social point of view, I had no choice but to go to underground clubs, where you didn't need to show ID, while I waited for my new passport to arrive. One evening, I was out dancing at one of these clubs in Crenshaw & Washington. I could see someone staring, and I thought he was interested in me, so I made a beeline for a J&B Whisky with water and lots of ice at the bar."

I couldn't help but interrupt, "Not your usual glass of champagne then?" I asked playfully.

"This was a joint that wouldn't have even known how to spell Veuve Clicquot, Jill," Aitch exclaimed, "yet alone serve me one! A J&B with water was what I always drank in these parts of L.A. Anyway, as I was enjoying my drink, a guy I hadn't noticed before came up to me and tapped me on the shoulder. 'Have you lost your passport?' he said. 'Yes', I replied, 'but how do you know about that?' 'Well, I found it,' he said, 'and I recognised you instantly across the dance floor.' He didn't actually have my passport on him at the time but we chatted and swapped phone numbers, and I ended up going over to his place to collect it a few days later."

It was the end of my haircut and Aitch was brushing me down and helping me off with my gown. I knew we didn't have much time left, but there was a story half told and I still had unanswered questions about Aitch's time in L.A.

Aitch helped me on with my coat, and as he did so I managed to get in one last question. "What were you doing when the earthquake hit L.A.?" I blurted out, realising he would have been there at the time.

Aitch hesitated, and I could have sworn he came close to blushing. Then he looked me straight in the eye, and in a kind of whisper he said, "I was having sex with the guy who found my passport."

We both knew the punchline and didn't need to say it out loud – the earth really had moved for Aitch that day! I walked out of the salon into the bright sunshine chuckling to myself unashamedly.

Money is resented, birth is envied, ability is distrusted, but manners are loved, because they are greedless, beautiful and flattering.

Villiers David,
   Advice to my Godchildren

FRENCH LESSONS

"This is the ammunition," Ben said, as he opened up the briefcase on his lap.

My heart was in my mouth as Aitch described his first trip on a plane. *What the hell was inside that briefcase*, I wondered, *for Ben to describe it in such a way?*

Before I had time to come up with my own answer, Aitch grinned at me with a knowing look. "It was a case full of money, Jill, thousands of crisp French francs just like out of a gangster movie."

I could instantly picture the scene and feel Aitch's nervous anticipation. He was flying to Paris with Ben who knew the city well, spoke French, and was planning to take Aitch to all the very best places, armed with a briefcase of cash. It felt exciting and dangerous. What had they got up to together? And how had this experience shaped Aitch's story?

By now, we had a routine. Once my hair had been washed, I would sit back while Aitch got to work with his scissors and started telling more stories from his life.

"We were staying at L'Hotel in Paris," Aitch began. "It was rather fitting really, as it turned out this was the hotel where Oscar Wilde stayed for several months without paying his bill, creating one hell of a scandal.

"The hotel was the ultimate in opulence," he went on. "It was circular, and quite amazingly had an aviary in the centre of its dining room with exotic birds flying around. The rooms were beautifully decorated with the finest Egyptian cotton sheets on the beds, shiny chrome taps, fluffy white towels and black marble bathrooms. It tasted of luxury."

Aitch licked his lips and I could tell that he could see and smell the place, and that he was conscious of how special being there had made him feel. "It was there that Ben introduced me to Roger and Gallet soaps or savons as he called them, the sort of soaps that give you a sense of well-being and luxury even in the simple act of washing your hands.

"I also started to learn about the art of refined perfume and discovered the sensory experiences it can create. Back in London, Ben and I used to love going to Floris in Jermyn Street to try different fragrances. Our two all-time favourites were Verbena essence and Stephanotis bath oil. Just talking about them brings back the sensations so vividly."

Aitch paused and I had a moment to reflect. Of course I'd seen Roger and Gallet products in expensive hotels, but they weren't the sorts of soap I'd ever bought as I considered them way too luxurious for day-to-day use. Aitch's description, however, made me think that maybe I was missing out.

"Ben and I led a dilettante lifestyle in Paris," Aitch said. "We would wander down to the Café Flor before dinner and sit on the pavement in our preferential seats. It was really a place to see and be seen, and Ben and I would stay there for hours drinking coffee, champagne and cognac. At first, I couldn't get used to seeing people drinking and eating outside," he said. "I'd never experienced that before but I quickly realised it was all part of the lifestyle, and", he said, beaming at me, "I got rather good at it. I watched and learnt from Ben. He was worldly, smart, but also caring and loving. He was attentive to me and I always felt safe with him. We both knew I was from a different class, but somehow he knew how to make me feel comfortable. I felt he was proud to be with me. I was part of a double act and wherever Ben wanted to go, I knew it was going to be fun. I could also tell that other people were fascinated by us. I would notice a prolonged visual enquiry in their eyes as we walked down the street, and Ben and I would look at each other knowingly. It made us feel good because we knew we were a handsome couple, and we liked to be noticed."

I tried to picture the young Aitch walking down the boulevards of Paris with Ben. What a striking couple they would have made – like a pair of colourful peacocks, with their heads held high. Ben, the quintessential English gentleman, with the instantly recognisable poise that a public school education provides; immaculately dressed and oozing charisma and charm, with a zest for life and an infectious laugh. And by his side, the young Aitch, with a quiet assurance all of his own, a desire to learn from Ben, and an insatiable curiosity to try new things.

Aitch had described to me how he liked to look like a Motown singer, with his toned torso provocatively on show under his fitted flowery shirt, and his Afro hairstyle blowing in the breeze. I could imagine them laughing their way down the street; Ben in his leather Gucci brogues and Aitch, (so he'd told me) in bright red platform shoes. They would have turned heads anywhere.

Ben and Aitch came from such different worlds, but something drew them to each other, and, as I was to discover, it was to become a relationship full of fun, excitement and glamour, tinged with a sense of sadness in the knowledge that it could not last forever.

There was a pause while Aitch looked at my hair and we both remembered why I was there. "Why don't we take it a little shorter today?" he said. "I believe there should always be some progression; a style shouldn't be maintained for too long."

I'd always taken such a conservative approach to my hair but by now I trusted Aitch implicitly and readily agreed. "Just make sure it still looks professional," I said, unable to disguise a little anxiety in my voice. I'd detected that Aitch was pushing for an edgier cut – as he got to know me better, he knew there was more to me than the professional image I showed to the world. But I wasn't quite ready for that yet.

"We would go shopping in the Rue Saint-Laurent," Aitch continued, as we returned to his story, "and it was there that Ben bought me my first Hermès belt and a pair of gorgeous Gucci shoes." I could see as he spoke how Aitch was starting to develop his style with a French sophistication that was both classy and classic, while making a statement in the way he put an outfit together and the way he wore it. He was curious and adventurous, trying out as many new experiences as he could with the enthusiasm of an ingénue, and starting to appreciate the finer things in life.

My mind had started to wander, and before I knew it Aitch was half way through the next chapter of his story about Paris. "Ben once asked me tenderly to close my eyes," he said, "as I did so he placed a silver spoon in my mouth. It had something on it that I didn't recognise but which had a horrid texture and taste to it. In fact, I found it so disgusting I spat it out – I was really quite revolted," he said. "It was only later that Ben told me it had been the finest Beluga caviar. He explained everything to me, from where it came from, to how it should be served with blinis, egg yolks, finely chopped scallions and crème fraiche. Of course, Jill," he announced, grinning from ear to ear, "over the years I've developed a real taste for Beluga and Sevruga caviar, and it's now one of my real passions. But that was my very first encounter with it."

I worried at times that other clients in the salon would overhear our conversation and be shocked by what we were talking about. But everyone seemed deep in their own more mundane exchanges, blissfully unaware of the deliciously risqué stories I was listening to. I sat enthralled, willing my haircut to last much longer than the usual hour.

"It was bordering on the insane," said Aitch, bringing me back to Paris. He was describing his visits to the Crazy Horse and the Moulin Rouge with Ben. "The shows were sexually very explicit," he said, with a wicked look in his eye, "but the French were pretty difficult to shock even when it was completely over the top. It had a sort of underground feeling to it. It was sinful, and I was having to learn to adapt to new things; it was a discovery of a different world and of myself."

As I indulged my imagination in the scene he was portraying, I felt a sense of complicity in the iniquity of it all, and I desperately wanted to know more.

"It had an essence of excited danger," he went on, "with the most provocative of costumes worn by both the men and the women. In fact, Jill, that's where I first became fascinated by leather."

Just then Aitch was called away to consult with one of the other stylists on a client's hair colour. I sat back and breathed deeply. I was starting to get to know Aitch, but he continuously surprised and amazed me. What had Ben and Aitch got up to in the clubs and bars of Paris in the '70s? And what did he mean about his fascination with leather? He gave me a tantalising glimpse into his lifestyle, but it was still full of unanswered questions, and I got the distinct impression that's how he liked it. Aitch was always a bit of a tease and he had a raunchy charisma, but it was all presented with hints and knowing looks that added to his charm.

When he returned to my side, Aitch continued his story but by now he had moved south from Paris. "We drove down to Cannes one time," he said, "in Ben's gold Rolls Royce of course. The car never lost its smell of new leather and the soft tan seats made me feel like I was sitting on a big comfy sofa. I remember feeling very happy as we headed down the autoroute singing along to Marvin Gaye's *What's Going On?* at the top of our voices. It was a time of complete abandon.

"When we got to Cannes," Aitch continued, "we stayed at the Hotel Martinez and I'd never seen such a large hotel before, yet alone one with its own private beach – a beach that had smart deckchairs laid out neatly in rows. They were really close together with tables between them to place your champagne glasses on. You had to navigate your way carefully around the tiny spaces between them to take up your place. It was also the first time in my life that I'd seen people putting sun cream on their bodies, and there was a smell of exotic lotions in the air that was new to me. I remember how wonderful I felt sitting under a parasol, my body oiled to perfection with Piz Buin. I've learnt, Jill," he said, "that even as a black man, some protection from the sun is key, and to this day I only use the best available sun oils."

"So what did you do on the beach?" I asked.

"Well, I made myself comfortable with my 'petit table'," Aitch said, "and I laid back listening to the sound of the waves, while the attentive young waiters served me steak tartare with pommes frites and Mateus rosé wine – the height of luxury in those days. To be honest with you, I didn't know before that moment that it was even possible to eat on a beach. It all seemed rather impractical at first, but I discovered everything was fine as long as you made sure the sand didn't get into your food. More importantly though, it made me feel so glamorous," Aitch sighed.

"The beach was full of young men posing in Speedos. They preened themselves in the hot Mediterranean sun against a background of yachts in the marina. Ben himself had a great physique from his days working out in the army, and I have to confess," Aitch said coquettishly, "he looked great in swimwear. He and I would meet up with friends for lunch and drink Campari soda or Harvey Wallbangers," he said. "Then we'd go to drag shows in the evenings. It was like being on the set of the *Cages aux Folles*," he laughed, "and Ben insisted on giving me a number of nicknames." Aitch hesitated, perhaps unsure as to whether to reveal such an intimate detail, but I wasn't going to let him deny me.

"Oh do tell," I said.

"Well, one of them was H bomb," he said, "and the other was Twinkle Toes".

I laughed out loud. "How marvellous," I replied, wondering how many other people were privy to this delicious information.

"It was a fabulous lifestyle," said Aitch, "quite different from anything I'd ever experienced before – a world full of convertibles cruising around, and champagne corks popping, with sexy people showing off their deeply tanned skin that had that distinctively divine smell that comes from the warmth of the sun. I also came to realise there were a lot of freeloaders there, or gigolos as they called themselves, hanging around gay bars waiting to be picked up by guys with money. Ben, however, was always very sensitive to my position. He didn't want anyone getting the wrong impression of me as a hanger-on or a gold digger. He took care of me, protecting me and teaching me at the same time, making me aware of what was going on. At one point, he even gave me all his cash and insisted that I paid for everything."

I looked at him in the mirror and Aitch realised he needed to explain. "You see, Jill, Ben wanted me to be treated with respect", he said, "to be his partner and to be seen to be so, and I really appreciated that. He taught me to anticipate things, to be prepared, and to know how to deal with situations with sensitivity so that no one was ever embarrassed. It's a lesson I've carried with me to this day.

"While we were in Cannes, Ben and I went to dinner at Tony Richardson's house just outside St. Tropez", Aitch continued. "In fact," he said, "we ended up staying for two whole days. He had a beautiful estate up in the hills and I remember Jody and Vanessa being there too, although Vanessa was obviously quite young then. There was a group of small houses and all the guests had their own accommodation. Ben and I would go down to the beach every morning for a few hours in the sun, before having lunch together at a local restaurant somewhere up in the hills. In the evening, we'd walk along the promenade and regularly bump into people Ben knew – of course, as you might imagine, there'd be some curiosity aroused in my direction on those occasions."

I could certainly believe that, I thought, as I imagined the two of them strolling in the balmy sunshine along the harbour at St. Tropez. I'd been there once and remembered it as *the* place to be seen.

"It was a wonderful time, and a beautiful place, with stunning vistas and a cool breeze that had a sense of tranquillity about it," said Aitch. "The trees cast a special sort of shadow in the sunshine and created all sorts of shapes on the road – it's a very special memory for me and it's how I always think of the South of France.

"From St. Tropez," Aitch continued, "we went on to Avignon and Aix-en-Provence and we played an awful lot of backgammon. I remember the squares and the fountains, and the taste of crème caramel and white Sambuca with coffee beans." The images Aitch summoned up were like an impressionist painting. As he talked, I could see the subtle colours of the Mediterranean light in my mind's eye, and I could sense a feeling of love and friendship in the shimmering heat.

I hesitated to break the spell that Aitch's story had created, but I wanted to find out what had eventually happened to Aitch's relationship with Ben.

"I was young and naïve in those days," Aitch sighed, as I prompted him to tell me. "Back in London, our usual arrangement was for Ben to ring me and then come and pick me up for lunch or dinner, or to meet up with friends. For some reason on one particular day, I decided to turn up unexpectedly at his place in Chelsea – and there he was with another young man. Of course, I should have realised it wasn't an exclusive relationship, but it hit me hard and I didn't deal with it well. It made me realise how much Ben meant to me; it was my first deep infatuation, and I recognised that, irrespective of my emotions, I was never going to have more than what I had from him. We sort of drifted apart after that. But we remained friends, and from time to time we would have dinner together. I've never forgotten how good he was to me. It was from Ben that I developed a hunger for adventure and living life to the full, and it was Ben who gave me the confidence to become the hunter rather the hunted."

"What do you mean?" I asked.

"Well," said Aitch, "my family would disagree – for them, my pedigree was already established – but through my experiences with Ben, I found a way of expressing my true self. I was liberated from the attitudes of my grandmother's generation."

"Did you see Ben again after that?" I asked. "Yes much later on, Jill, I did," he said, quietly. "By that time, our respective fortunes were quite different. Ben had fallen on hard times and so on this occasion, it was me taking him out to dinner. We went to the Albany Courtyard in Piccadilly, which had always been a favourite of ours. I wanted to show Ben what I'd become thanks to the education he'd given me early on in my life. And I wanted to repay his generosity to me in a small way.

"Ben refined my life," Aitch said, looking me firmly in the eye. "From him, I learnt the proper way of doing things; I learnt how to present myself and to hold myself with pride and confidence. I owe him a lot." Aitch stopped speaking and I could tell that this was a moment of sad reflection for him. The bravado had disappeared and his eyes were tinged with sadness.

"And what became of Ben?" I asked tentatively.

"Sadly, he died," Aitch replied. "I found out from a friend of his who'd been wrapping Christmas presents with him towards the end. He rang me to say that Ben had talked fondly of Twinkle Toes in the final days of his life, and that I'd always held a special place in his heart and he invited me to his funeral. I was pleased to be there and I turned up proudly to pay my respects. It amused me to see the other guests who'd turned up, many of whom I'd met over the years. There were all the other boyfriends of course, some of them acknowledged me and others were rather more reserved, but I think it would have amused and pleased Ben to see us all there."

Despite Aitch's lighthearted comment, I felt a lump in my

throat. He looked at me in the mirror with his deep brown eyes and we both knew how much this had meant. As he brushed the hair from my shoulders and took me across to retrieve my coat, a silence fell between us as we both reflected on the story and its significance. I felt privileged to have heard it, and I hoped it had not pained Aitch too much to tell me. I walked out on to the street in a thoughtful mood and hailed a cab back to the office.

Use a spoon for rice

Villiers David,
     Advice to my Godchildren

ART ON A PLATE

I was lucky enough to be in a position where I could nip out to the hairdressers any time in the day. I had control of my own diary, but with all the travel and meetings I had, it was often difficult to find an hour and a half when I could fit it in. On one famous occasion some years previously, I'd managed to escape to the hairdresser's mid-afternoon. The shampoo had just been massaged into my hair, when the receptionist came over and told me that my secretary was on the phone. This was most unusual and rather alarming. I crept to the phone with a towel on my head, only to learn that the senior partner had just rung her and wanted to see me straight away. My loyal secretary had not told him where I was, but I needed to get back to the office immediately. So I made my apologies to the stylist, towel dried my shampoo-filled hair as best I could, and ran in my high heels back to the office. Quite what the senior partner had made of me as I stood in front of him with my hair glued to my scalp and slightly out of breath, thankfully I will never know, but it had made me nervous ever since about attending appointments during the day. So I tended to go during lunchtime if I could. The downside was I ended up sitting there, as I was today, totally famished.

It wasn't helping that Aitch was talking about his latest extravagant dinner party in mouth-watering detail. "We started with an amuse-bouche of parsnip and parmesan cheese with black pepper and croutons," he said, "followed by salted fishcakes with smoked mackerel soufflé, garnished with twigs of fresh thyme and watercress, and accompanied by a Mediterranean cucumber mousse with green, red and yellow peppers and homemade rosemary bread – you get me?" I just loved the way that Aitch described food in such a way that you could almost taste it. He had a complete lexicon just for the taste and colours of food that he deliciously brought to life. I could picture him preparing his dinner parties with close attention to detail, and taking great delight in entertaining his guests with his inimitable flamboyant style.

"The main course was trout with roasted tomatoes that I stuffed with Brie, garlic, thyme, red peppers and mushrooms, and served with peppercorns, black beans, sweet plantains, sweetcorn and spinach," he continued.

It sounded like a real feast, and I could tell how Aitch applied his creativity to the menu by drawing on all those meals he'd enjoyed in French restaurants, and the Chelsea dinner parties he'd been to with Ben. Aitch's early experiences with food included steak tartare, caviar and exquisite canapés. His education was certainly being put to good use now.

I'd noticed how open Aitch was to trying new things. He had a natural curiosity and a sense of adventure that was reflected in the twinkle in his eye. He experimented with food and menus just like he did with other aspects of his life. It had all clearly started with Ben sharing the finer things in life with him. It was Ben who'd introduced Aitch to gentleman's relish from Fortnum and Mason that the two of them used to eat on toast, and Ben who'd taken him to eat at the finest and most famous restaurants of the day, such as the Pietro di Monzi on the Fulham Road, San Lorenzo's in Beauchamp Place and the Brasserie St Quentin on the Brompton Road. Aitch had described to me how he'd taken afternoon tea at Claridges, and how he'd eaten at Mr Chow's restaurant in Knightsbridge in the days when Chinese food was considered exotic.

"Mr Chow's was frequented by all the A-list celebrities," he explained. "It was full of models and Sloane Rangers, of course, but for me it was a whole new experience. I remember the first time I saw chopsticks – I had absolutely no idea how to use them, but I didn't want to embarrass myself, especially as my skill is all about using my hands. So I watched and carefully copied what everyone else did, until I got the hang of it."

It was interesting to hear how food had been such a socialising thread to Aitch's time with Ben. It struck me that these experiences had taught Aitch a whole lot more than how to use chopsticks.

"The food I serve is designed like a piece of art on a plate," Aitch said. "It's really important to get the presentation right. I aim for everything to be pristine and perfectly placed. It's about making a statement – having the confidence to expose yourself in that way, and to be remembered for it. At my dinner parties, I serve each course on my best Villeroy and Boch plates, and I take time before my guests arrive to dress the table with flowers, beautiful glasses and the best linen napkins."

It wasn't a surprise. Aitch always paid close attention to detail, and he had a naturally artistic eye – he wouldn't be satisfied until his dining table looked immaculate and very very stylish.

"For dessert, I prepared peaches in honey with caramelised pineapple, blueberries, pomegranate seeds and vanilla ice cream garnished with fresh mint, black sugar and cinnamon sticks," Aitch said.

We were back to the description of his latest dinner party menu, and I was salivating at the sound of it.

"I served dessert on individual slabs of black slate," he said, with the outline shape of a fork and spoon on each. I looked quizzically at Aitch in the mirror and he quickly explained further. "I sprinkled the cutlery with icing sugar," he said, "and left the impression on the black background. It was quite stunning."

"That's amazing," I said, "what a great idea." It was something I would never have thought of doing myself, but I could instantly see how effective it must have looked.

"Funnily enough," said Aitch, "I got the idea from a really mediocre meal I once had in Tenerife. I was sitting in the restaurant of a pretty awful hotel on my own after Donald and I had had a row and I decided to have dinner on my own. We made up later, even although I'd already had my dessert, but one can be inventive, if you know what I mean?" he said, with a wicked smile that suggested something quite decadent had taken place.

"I seem to remember I was the only person in the restaurant that night, but despite that the service was terrible. It was one of those meals you just want to get over with, or that's how I was feeling until I ordered dessert and to my surprise, it arrived on a piece of slate. The presentation of the white icing sugar outlining where the cutlery would have been against the black background was quite spectacular and it immediately lifted my spirits," he said. *It was so like Aitch*, I thought, *to have been inspired like that, to pick up a creative idea from such an unlikely source, and to follow it through so meticulously to recreate it himself.* "When I got home, I went down to a tile shop in Colindale," he explained, "to find some black slate, and then I experimented until I got the trick with the icing sugar just right." I made a secret mental note to try this for myself at my next dinner party.

The food Aitch cooked was clearly full of colour and taste and beautifully presented. I was savouring it as I sat in the chair listening to him talking about his experiences with food.

"When you grow up in the Caribbean," Aitch explained, "spices are part of your DNA. I'm fascinated by condiments, by the way spices can be combined to create different flavours, and how I can use a full palette of colours on the plate. In Dominica, there's freshly cooked food everywhere – it's all organic, of course, and it's cooked in hot stoves and served from street stalls that look like little beach huts along the side of the roads. I love the way the chefs there work in the tiniest of kitchens to produce such fabulous food and to make a business out of it too. You need a strong entrepreneurial spirit to

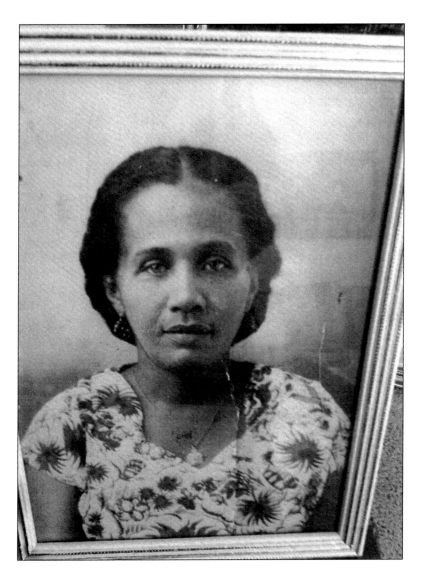

Margaret, my beloved grandmother

Sweet sixteen in London

Reflections at a villa in Aix-en-Provence

Shipwreck in Tangiers

As a young man in Los Angeles

Aitch makes his mark in Japan

From top left: Platform work in Manila; Seminar in Jamaica; Royal Albert Hall show; Close up concentration; With model in Japan; With model in Manila; Creative gents cut.

Creative salon and session images: Short Mouche Afro; Glamorous punk; Tribal Couture; Soft Afro.

Working with celebrities. From top left: Jody Watley; Summer in the city collection L.A., Faye Dunaway; Summer in the city collection; Emma Soames; The Butler & Wilson campaign; Melanie Sykes; Devine.

From top left: Tracey Ullman with 2 Emmys; First lady of the Philippines with Vidal; Jerry Hall; Debbie Allen; Saffron Burrows and Lorraine Pascale; At a couture show; In traditional costume, Japan.

From top left: Aitch's blond ambition; At a press conference; With Vidal, Ronnie, Mary Quant and Emmanuelle Khanh; Attending to a debutante wedding; The cast of A Different World.

From top left: World class tribute, Manila; In Jamaica – Awards ceremony; hands on with models, posing in cutting gowns, delighted students.

make food successfully in a space no bigger than a cupboard," he laughed, "and I really admire that."

"Tell me about the food you had as a boy," I said.

"For sure," Aitch replied, "the food was quite simple but absolutely delicious. We had dasheens, christophenes, plantains, sweet potatoes, yams, cassava and avocados – all beautifully served in the exquisite glass collection that my grandmother had acquired from Guadeloupe over the years. In fact, that's where my own fascination with glass started. As a young boy, I used to sit mesmerised by the light reflected in the different coloured glasses in her display cabinet, and I've recreated that same effect with my own collection at home.

"You need to understand, Jill," said Aitch, "that in my family, food is something to sustain you, not just to satisfy your hunger. If my siblings or I haven't seen my mum for a while, she always feeds us. It's a kind of show of love, and it's my mum's humble way of showing it. Her whole essence is for us to eat together, and we all know it's a sign of healing too."

It was deep stuff but spoken with great sincerity. Food, however simple, was important to relationships, and Aitch had learnt this as a young child. Now as a grown man he used food in the same way, but always with extraordinary style, and much more adventurously.

"I like to see the salon dressed for special occasions too," Aitch continued excitedly, "and food has become a really important part of that. On one occasion, one of the major banks hired the salon for their clients on Valentine's Day and I hired Kristopher Robert-Jude to dress the place, and it was just glorious – he's so incredibly gifted. From him, I learnt how to place blueberries, raspberries, fresh mint and pomegranate seeds around each position, and to sprinkle black sugar crystals from Fortnum and Mason to make everything sparkle in the candlelight. Oh, and I usually add some grated nutmeg too – it gives out such a delicious aroma that fills the salon."

I sat back and closed my eyes and could have sworn that I could smell nutmeg and taste raspberry juice on my lips. I was in a kind of food heaven when I heard Aitch's voice again.

"One of my greatest food passions," he said, "is eating al fresco. I remember the very first time I experienced it. It was when Ben and I went to dinner at Barbara Hutton's house in Tangiers. When we got there, we were led up to a roof terrace where a sumptuous dinner table had been laid out under the stars. I couldn't believe it. It was a really really hot day and the whole experience had something of *The Great Gatsby* about it – eating off starched white linen in the moonlight with candles and champagne. And then, of course, there were those equally wonderful occasions when Ben and I would end up dining on the pavement of the Champs Elysée or taking lunch on the beach at Cannes."

"Eating outdoors creates its own special atmosphere," he went on, "a kind of simple decadence, but it has to be done in style. I absolutely adore picnics, but I won't sit on the grass and I never ever drink out of plastic cups," he said disdainfully.

"I used to cut the hair of André Previn and Simon Rattles' wives and it was from them that I first heard all about Glyndebourne and the picnic tradition," he went on. "Once I'd been there for myself, I knew the English way was the only way to do a picnic. Donald and I put a great deal of effort and joy in preparing all the glorious food and packing up half our home in baskets – or at least as much of it as we can carry," he laughed.

"I try to make every picnic a Glyndebourne experience", he continued. "One of the best was a picnic I hosted at Kenwood House at the Motown 50th anniversary concert. The theme was white on white with glass and silver. We found a perfect space on the lawn and I dressed it like a five star restaurant. I made sure there was loads of ice to chill the champagne, water and juices. And I dressed the picnic spot with designer cushions, pristine white linen napkins with napkin rings, a decanter, crystal ashtrays and fresh red roses in Lalique vases. Then I drizzled everything in rose water.

"We started by sipping champagne from delicate champagne flutes and then we gorged ourselves on smoked salmon, caviar and fresh scallops; all served on the best porcelain Wedgwood plates. We made quite an impact and people came over just to take a look and photograph us. It was a memorable occasion enjoyed by everyone who'd come, especially to listen to Motown music – music that never fails to uplift me with its beat. I loved every moment of it."

My haircut was almost done, and I knew I was going to have to find something to eat on the way back to the office to allow me to concentrate back at work. It was likely to be a sandwich and a piece of fruit – a poor substitute for the sort of food I was now dreaming of. Aitch brushed the hair from my shoulders and gave me a tissue to wipe my face. He looked at me to check everything was okay.

"It looks great", I said. "Thank you so much, and good luck with your next dinner party. I know how much hard work goes into them."

"Well thank god for Wendy, that's all I can say," Aitch replied.

"Wendy?" I asked, as I took out my purse to pay for my haircut.

"Wendy," he said with a flourish, as he strode towards his next client, "is the name I gave to my dishwasher."

To stare wistfully at the tiny flower-bed of your youth, while in every direction the earth and sky teem with untried novelties is to confess yourself contemptibly unimaginative.

Villiers David,
                Advice to my Godchildren

MY GRANDMOTHER'S WISDOM

As I sat on the sofa watching the opening ceremony of the Olympics, I knew I was the only one in the room waiting to see if Dominica were fielding a team. London was buzzing with the Olympics. There had been all sorts of last minute crises surrounding security and transport and strikes, but at last the whole country seemed ready to sit back and enjoy this moment in history.

I was at my friend Libby's house with a whole group of people watching the opening ceremony with glasses of Pimms, and there was a real party atmosphere. We'd all been wowed by Danny Boyle's spectacular show that had made us laugh and cry, but most of all be very proud to be British. In the midst of the hubbub I was thinking of Aitch. He was so patriotic, he loved the Royals, especially the Queen, and I felt sure that he'd be watching the opening ceremony too with a personal sense of national pride. But his native country was Dominica, and although I'd been to the Caribbean a few times, it was an island I knew very little about.

I waited as the teams of athletes appeared for their parade around the arena. It was getting close, Denmark, Djibouti and then, sitting on the edge of my seat, and straining to hear above the party noise, I heard the team being announced: "Dominica, Isle of Beauty, Isle of Splendour," boomed the announcer. "One of the loveliest unspoilt islands in the Caribbean." I had no doubt that Aitch, his mum, his aunty Shirley and the rest of the Peters family would be cheering loudly at this point, and I let out a quiet cheer unheard by anyone around me, to acknowledge the moment.

Aitch had referred to Dominica a couple of times in our conversations, but I wanted to find out more about his origins; they'd clearly had a big impact on him, and I was curious to find out more about his family and his early life before he came over to England. *What was it like living in Dominica,* I wondered, *and how did he cope as a young boy arriving in London in the 1950s?*

When I arrived at the salon a few days later, Aitch was in buoyant mood. As usual, he approached me as I sat in reception with a broad smile and a warm embrace.

"So lovely to see you again Jill," he said with his usual sincerity.

As it happened, Aitch had just finished one of his paintings and he was keen to show it to me on his ipad. As with all of his paintings, it was remarkable for its vibrancy.

"This one's called African Bush Fire," he said proudly. I remarked on the wonderful colours, and as luck would have it he immediately related them to the Caribbean, "the reds and oranges are just like the colour of the landscape set against the azure blue sky," he explained wistfully. "And then there are the wonderful flavours that the colours summon up – the smell of smoked meat and crab backs cooking, and of burning tyres, and the salt in the wind from the sea."

This, I could tell, was my moment.

"Tell me more about Dominica," I urged.

"For sure," Aitch said, looking at me intently for a moment in the mirror, and then lowering his eyes as his story began. "Dominica is a spice island," he said with a quiet pride, "with an unusual landscape. It's full of abundance and lovely warm-hearted people. A lot of the vegetation has medicinal values and the women grow up learning from their mothers and grandmothers how to make bush teas, and how to use herbs to treat illnesses. There's even a special type of frog on the island that's supposed to make you live longer if you eat enough of it. That's why people from Dominica live so long and why we all look so good – allegedly," Aitch said, grinning from ear to ear.

I wasn't sure if he was kidding me but it was a good story and the looking good bit was certainly true of Aitch himself. He guarded the secret of his precise age carefully, but I suspected he looked a lot younger than he really was.

"My grandmother lived until she was ninety-nine," Aitch continued, "even though she'd had a hard life as a young widow with eight kids, one of whom tragically passed away. I never met my grandfather, but I know he was a big shot on the island, and when he died my grandmother was left to find a way of feeding all the kids. She took in lodgers and she sewed a lot: dresses, trousers, anything that she could sell. She came from Guadeloupe and she would go there regularly to sell the clothes she'd made, and to bring things back to sell in Dominica. People were pretty poor on the island as you might expect, Jill, but most of them had made-to-measure wardrobes thanks to my grandmother!" he laughed.

"Tell me more about her," I urged. "She sounds like a remarkable woman."

"Thank you, Jill," Aitch said, "I believe she was in so many ways. Some of my most vivid memories of her are the sound of fabric tearing and the thud of scissors on the wooden kitchen table. I could tell from each particular sound whether she was threading a bobbin, cutting fabric or sewing on her precious Singer sewing machine. My grandmother was very creative, you see, and she could make any kind of outfit from scratch. She also loved using exotic fabrics and embellishing them with lace and unusual trimmings, much to the pleasure of her customers."

"I guess," said Aitch, looking up at me as though the thought had only just occurred to him, "that's where my fascination with fabric and fashion originally came from, and it's probably also how I learnt to be creative with my hands. My grandmother had a lot of strength and determination; a sense of accomplishment was important to her. When I look back now and reflect on my family roots, I can see how her strength and single-minded independence are part of my genes. It's something we all share; it's in our spirit."

"So your grandmother was a really big influence in your life?" I asked.

"For sure," Aitch replied. "My mother came to London on her own when I was a small boy and worked really hard to start a new life for us all. When she left Dominica, I went to live with my grandmother, and I used to go to school every day with my aunty Shirley who was the youngest of her children.

"My grandmother was a strict catholic and that meant going to church a lot, not just on Sundays but after school as well. I liked going to church but mostly, if I'm honest, I went because there was a chance of getting a glass of lemonade. I always looked forward to that. I used to go to Bible classes too because they served refreshments – I guess food was already pretty important to me," Aitch laughed.

"Although I realise now that attending church regularly as a child had more of an impact on me than I realised for a long time. There was a level of discipline involved that's stayed with me, and my religion has given me a strong moral compass. I always do the sign of the cross as I pass the church in the car on my way to see my mum in Kenton on a Sunday, saying my three Our Fathers and ten Hail Marys. I try to complete my prayers before I get to her front door, although on some occasions," he tittered, "my prayers get jeopardised by the traffic lights."

I smiled as I thought of Aitch swerving through the streets of north London determined to get through his devotions.

"I remember being part of the procession to church as a boy," Aitch continued, "and the wonderful candles, not just normal size candles but the huge altar ones that seemed to rise up from the floor and were taller than I was. They created peace, serenity and a sort of romance throughout the church. I've never lost my fascination with candles; the command and presence they bring to a room; the soft forgiving light they give, and that instantly recognisable smell. It all meant that I was brought up pretty strictly. There were certain things you definitely could or couldn't do. But, to be fair, my grandmother also gave me a lot of advice, which has stood me in good stead throughout my life. I try to abide by it even today."

"What sort of advice?" I asked.

"She told me to be proud of myself and to stand tall," Aitch replied. "To always do my very best and to hold my head high. She would tell me that dogs should be kept apart from doctors" – I looked quizzically, and Aitch explained – "I learnt that I should never be overfamiliar, but keep a respectable distance. As I child, of course, it meant that the adults wanted to talk and that was my signal to leave the room. But it was also a lesson in discretion and much later on I discovered that with discretion I could put my clients at ease. I gave them respect and demonstrated my ability to listen, just like my grandmother had taught me. Her advice came from a sense of enduring intent. She wanted me to be the very best I could be."

There was a pause almost as if Aitch's grandmother was standing right there admonishing him. Then Aitch beamed at me in the mirror. "Trust me girlfriend," he said. "I don't always get it right, but I sure as hell try."

It was easy to see how fond Aitch had been of his grandmother as he resumed his story. "My family were well-regarded in Dominica and, partly because my grandmother had so many children, we were pretty well known. It's a small island but we had a certain status, and a family reputation for integrity and humility. My grandmother was a proud woman and had a certain way of carrying herself. Everyone knew who she was and they respected her and would go to her for help. We lived in the capital Roseau and our house was quite large by local standards. It had a big veranda out front and beautiful wooden floors inside, with a shower in the back garden, and an outside toilet that bordered onto our neighbours."

"Tell me more about the island," I said, aware of my own ignorance. "What's it like?"

"There's some very interesting geography," Aitch replied. "One side of Dominica is volcanic and has sandy beaches. It's like something out of *Robinson Crusoe*, with wide sweeping bays and lovely almond trees. Sadly though," he said, looking at me over the rim of his glasses, "when I was growing up there were no sun loungers or fit young waiters serving lunch and iced cocktails on the beaches there.

"The rural part of the island is in the centre," he went on. "As kids, we used to describe the people who visited us from there as 'up from the wood', and believe me it wasn't meant as a compliment. There was a surprising amount of snobbery and class distinction on the island about who you were and where you lived. My grandparents on my father's side lived in the country and sometimes I would go for the school holidays – but I hated it," Aitch said, pulling a face.

"Why was that?" I asked.

"Well, I was always in shorts and my legs would get scratched to pieces as I walked through the long grass in the countryside. And I was scared stiff of the snakes that lurked there," Aitch said, visibly shivering at the memory of it. "Of course," he continued, "I learnt to love country life later on but only, you understand, if I can stay at a grand country house and there's no prospect of having to walk in the long grass."

I smiled at his snobbishness, learnt initially in those early days as a child, cemented by the time he spent with Ben and the English aristocracy, and reinforced by the people he'd met socially through his clients.

Aitch smiled at my quiet amusement. "My childhood was really a very happy time," he said with feeling. "I was the first born grandchild and I guess I was pretty spoilt. Despite my grandmother's circumstances we were never short of food and my school uniform was always pressed immaculately. We even had servants, but that really wasn't that unusual for families like mine. Of course, there were no washing machines, and certainly no 'Wendys' to help out, so everything was done by hand and the servants typically did the laundry and took care of the garden."

"What language is spoken on the island?" I asked, realising again how little I knew, but aware that for Aitch there was a clearly pride in talking about his home country.

"Dominica was originally a French colony," he replied, "and so a French patois is spoken as well as English, although in my family that wasn't encouraged when I was a child."

So that explained how Aitch had been at ease on that first trip to Paris, I thought. There was a French influence to his origins that had served him well. "What about the rest of your family?" I asked.

"I didn't know much about my dad," Aitch replied. "He was already playing around by the time I came along, but I was very close to my mum – and I still am," he said smiling broadly.

How I would love to meet Aitch's mum, I thought. She was clearly quite a remarkable lady having left her family to start a new life in London at a time when segregation might not have been officially sanctioned but was still pretty prevalent. It couldn't have been at all easy for her as a single working mother.

As if reading my mind, Aitch started talking more about his mother. "My mum came to London at the time of the Teddy boy riots," he said. "It was extremely hard to rent a house as a black woman with kids in those days, and it was a very difficult time for her. But I can see now how resilient it made her. She was always a strong woman, but her experience when she arrived here made her even stronger. Thankfully, she wasn't alone for long. My sister was the first to join her in London, followed by my other sister and then my brother."

"What about you?" I asked.

"As the eldest son, I had to wait 'til last," he said. "It was common in those days for families to get together and pool their money until there was enough to pay for the passage of one child. So we came over one at a time. My mum's never approved of HP; she always paid cash – so it took a while before all five of us were back together. In fact, it was only mum's carefulness with money that got us all over here," he said, pausing momentarily. "I only wish I'd inherited that from her, but my tendency is to spend rather than save."

He looked at me with a wry smile. I could see the naughty child within him, and could imagine his mother's exasperation with her son's spending habits.

"Although my mum does share my passion for buying shoes," he exclaimed, as if to point out that his mum did have at least one spending weakness.

"Is your father still alive?" I asked tentatively, wondering what had happened to the rest of the family in the years since Aitch had left for England.

"Yes he is," said Aitch. "In fact, I met him only a couple of years ago. It was the first time I'd been back to Dominica for twenty-seven years and my sister suggested I went. My father's pretty old and it was a trip designed to say goodbye to him I guess. As it happened, my niece became pregnant and her wedding was brought forward so I was able to join the family for that while I was over there."

"What was it like meeting your father after all that time?" I asked.

"I have to tell you, Jill, I was very nervous about seeing him again after so many years," Aitch replied. "I wanted to present myself in a certain way, and more than anything I wanted him to be proud of me. You see, hairdressing was never regarded very highly on the island, and I wanted my father to appreciate how successful I'd become in my chosen profession. Things have changed a lot since I was a boy. Nowadays, there's much more of an acceptance of the creative professions in Dominica; many young men have become successful chefs, florists, choreographers and even wedding planners, but in my day it just wasn't the done thing, and my father disapproved of me becoming a hairdresser."

"So how did it go?" I asked, slightly nervous on Aitch's behalf. "I took my sister and my niece with me for moral support," he said, "and we arrived at the house together. As I came into the room, my father stood up slowly to greet me. We embraced, but to be honest with you, I didn't really connect with him. I guess in my heart I was hoping he'd say how proud of me he was. But somehow that was never going to happen. Maybe I was wrong to even hope for it. He wasn't around in my early years to have any real appreciation of just how far I've come."

"Did you see anything of yourself in him?" I asked.

"Not really," Aitch replied thoughtfully, "but he was a very stylish man in his day, and I guess that's been his legacy to me."

There was a silence and I could sense how disappointed Aitch had been with the encounter with his father even at this late stage in their lives. He'd always wanted to make his father proud, but he'd left without any loving recognition of his success.

Then Aitch smiled at me as he continued. "I also bumped into my uncle Conrad while I was there," he said. "I had this childhood memory of him as dark-skinned and strong with a muscular physique. He used to work in the fields all day and to me as a young child he seemed like a kind of gladiator. Now, of course, in his old age he's all concave, but he's still got a wicked sense of humour, and we had a great time retelling family stories from the past. He has a joie de vivre and a cackling laugh that made me think of Ben. He also reminded me of the wonder and honesty that families from the countryside in Dominica always have – with none of the snobbishness that surrounded me when I was growing up in Roseau."

"Do you think you'll ever go back to Dominica?" I asked.

"I don't know," said Aitch, pensively. "It's a long way to go and it's expensive to get there. If I do go back again, it'd be purely for a holiday. I'd stay in the best hotel on the island overlooking the bay; I'd eat my breakfast on the terrace and I'd get my lunch from one of the street vendors selling dasheens – a real treat, for sure.

"My dream would be to build a house over there," Aitch continued wistfully. "I have a clear vision of how I'd design it on several different levels and with lots of reflective glass. I'd build a quiet courtyard in the centre and grow flowers there, and I'd create an ethereal atmosphere throughout. It would be heavily influenced by the images of all the wonderful places I still have in my mind from my travels around the world – the hotels, luxury spas and the fabulous personal homes I've stayed in over the years."

Aitch paused and I could tell he was reflecting on his grand design and processing the disappointment he'd felt in that final encounter with his father – if only his father could have seen him on that fancy hotel terrace or in his purpose-built island home.

Given the obvious emotion in the air, I decided to bring the conversation back to England. "How old were you when you left Dominica?" I asked.

"I came over here when I was around ten or eleven," Aitch replied. "At first, I didn't miss my mum too much because she used to send me wonderful parcels full of the latest fashions from London. Even then I was the best dressed boy in town," he beamed, "but when I knew I was coming to the UK, I was very excited. I remember sailing on this enormous ship for about three weeks before we eventually arrived at Southampton. I was chaperoned on the long journey by a family friend who was also emigrating to England and as we got off the train at Paddington station, there was a lot of hubbub and steam. It was all very different from the simple island life I was used to. From there, we travelled to Notting Hill Gate where my family were living in a small terraced house owned by Mrs Burns – our formidable Irish landlady. It was strange for me to see so many white kids everywhere, but I guess I wasn't nearly as curious about them as they were about me. It sort of set me apart at an early age."

"Of course, it wasn't easy," Aitch went on. "My mum had two or three jobs on the go all the time. She was a qualified nurse but she also did cleaning jobs to put food on the table for us all. She's a kind and generous person, so sometimes she would neglect her own family to take care of her patients – especially the older ones with no family of their own. I still remember the childish disappointment I felt one Christmas when mum put the turkey in the oven and went out to look after them, leaving my brother and sisters and I to take care of ourselves until she got back."

Aitch paused, and I could tell that he saw things differently now, and perhaps regretted how he'd reacted to his mum back then. "We've always been a close-knit family," he continued, "so when my younger brother died, it hit us all really hard." Aitch stopped abruptly, as if shaken by his own words.

I looked at him directly in the mirror. "Your brother died?" I repeated. "What happened?"

"Well," said Aitch, "it was all a big shock. I was in my early 20s and about to go on holiday to the Bahamas when I got the news. My brother had been complaining of headaches for a while and then one day he passed out at the bus stop. He was rushed to hospital, and stayed there for three to four months, diagnosed with sickle-cell anaemia. He never came home or recovered – and I don't think my mum ever properly recovered either. You see, Jill, my mum's never been one to complain and she dismisses anything to do with counselling, but I realise now how traumatic losing a child must have been. I've found throughout my life that it's only through talking things through with other people that you really get to understand your emotions and how deeply damaging they can be. I feel desperately sorry that my mum's never had any relief from that – if there is any to be had."

It was time for a break in the conversation and Aitch excused himself for a few minutes. When he returned, I was concerned about whether I'd probed too hard on the more painful memories from his early years. I needn't have worried as Aitch gave me one of his warm smiles, and I brought the conversation back to his grandmother.

"Did you learn anything else from her?" I asked.

"Well, Jill," he said, taking a deep breath and trying unsuccessfully to stifle a giggle, "when I was about five or six, my grandmother did insist on dressing me up as a girl in full national costume and marched me down the street for everyone to see. I was trying desperately not to be self-conscious because I knew she wouldn't have approved of that, so I held my head high and swished my skirts, which seemed to cause some amusement. Goodness knows what affect that experience had on me," he said with a playful flourish.

I was laughing so loudly by now that some of the other clients in the salon looked round to see what was happening. They'd missed the wonderful tales of Dominica and the hilarious punchline to Aitch's final story. That was mine to savour all afternoon as I returned to my desk.

*Education is using every means and taking
every personal risk to discover for yourself
what you can do best*

Villiers David,
Advice to my Godchildren

CONQUERING FEARS

I'd built a reputation over the years for being self-controlled and calm at work – I was difficult to read, some people would say, as I showed little of what I was really thinking. But I wasn't unhappy with that description. It was all to do with my early training when I'd been taught that being a consummate professional precluded the showing of emotion.

So I was surprised when Aitch looked at me in the mirror and asked, "What's upset you today Jill?"

I tried to brush the question off dismissively, but Aitch wasn't so easily put off. "Your head is hot, what's bothering you?" he persisted.

I was actually having a pretty awful day one way or another and despite my well-practised efforts to disguise my feelings, Aitch had instantly detected that something was wrong. I was struck by his ability to pick up on the slightest nuance by putting his hands on someone's head, and by his sensitivity to his clients' feelings.

As we started to talk, my stress started to ease. Aitch just had this way of relaxing you: the small touches to your shoulders, the gentleness in his voice and the expressiveness in his hands as he ran them through your hair, created a sense of calm and serenity. I felt able to talk to him about what was going wrong in my day. I found myself explaining to him how I'd learnt to hide my true feelings from those around me at work, in an attempt to convince them that everything was under control. I wasn't sure, I confessed, whether it was always the best policy.

A little to my surprise, Aitch immediately empathised with my dilemma. "It's very similar to my own experience," he said. "You have to learn to leave your problems at the salon door, and adopt the persona your clients expect of you. That's not always easy, but I was taught to give my clients my full attention, and that's what I do. What I don't really know is what that deprives you of?"

Aitch looked deeply serious and I realised that for once he was letting his salon persona slip to reveal some of his own inner feelings.

"What people don't realise," he said, "is that I have to cope every day with the impact that living with an alcoholic has on my emotional life, and I have to bury those feelings when I come into the salon. Last night's a good example. I went to a support meeting and there was a lot of soul-searching. It became clear that a lot of the time when I've been trying to help Donald, I've enabled him to avoid the consequences of his actions in a way I never intended. He knows that no matter how much he screws up, I'll always be there to rescue him. It's not an easy conclusion to accept, but I have to put all those thoughts to one side when I meet my clients."

I felt privileged to hear about Aitch's personal difficulties and I could see how hard he'd tried not to let his feelings show in all the times I'd met him at the salon. It struck me that a hair stylist was a bit like a psychotherapist, listening to clients, absorbing their moods and preoccupations, but remaining focused on making them feel good or better about themselves, no matter what was going on in their own lives.

It didn't seem like the time or the place to explore this further, but I needed to reassure Aitch that as far as I was concerned his professionalism triumphed over his inner feelings.

"I can't imagine you ever being stressed," I said, "especially at work; you're always so in control and at ease".

"I can see why you would say that, Jill," Aitch replied, "but it hasn't always been the case. Early on in my career, I often faced new and difficult situations that made me anxious or put me under a lot of pressure. For example, when I was living in Los Angeles, I was invited to go to Jamaica for a week to run a series of workshops. They were sponsored by Richardson-Vicks who wanted to promote their hair styling products in the Caribbean. By then, I'd already run lots of seminars in the States and in London, so I accepted the invitation quite readily. Up until that point, my confidence was assured."

"But when it came to going down there, I was really quite fearful. I suddenly realised this was a whole new situation. I was this young black hairdresser going from laid-back L.A. to Kingston, Jamaica — a place with a reputation for being pretty hard-core. I knew there was very little tolerance of gay guys on the island, and that there were no male hairstylists there at all. I was really worried that there would be hostility towards me, and I felt quite stressed out as I set off on the trip."

"How did it go?" I asked, certain that Aitch would have somehow found a way to win people over to him.

"Well, I was put up at The Pegasus," he said, "one of the best hotels in Kingston at the time. Thankfully, a Jamaican client of mine who used to come over to London twice a year knew I was coming over and she chaperoned me for the first few days until I felt safe and comfortable. She arranged for drinks and flowers in my hotel room which was sweet of her and made me feel really welcome. I do love hotel rooms, their luxury and comfort and the fact that I can drop wet towels on the floor and live in complete disorder to be able to have a clear head."

I smiled quietly at Aitch's remembrance. When he told his stories it was always the hotels he'd stayed in that seemed to make the biggest impact on him, and now I understood why.

"The first thing I had to do was to meet the models for the demonstrations that were planned to take place," he continued, "in a shopping mall of all places. I was very nervous about how it would go, but desperate not to let my anxiety show. As it happened, I needn't have worried because as soon as I met the models I felt so much better. The girls couldn't have been friendlier towards me, and I knew instinctively that everything was going to be okay. In fact, over the course of the week they allowed me to express my creativity in so many different ways. The trip turned out to be one of the best experiences in my professional life – and when I analyse it, I think it was principally because of the strength of my initial fears and how they were overcome."

"Tell me more," I prompted, as Aitch hesitated, unsure whether to continue or not.

"I worked closely with the organiser who'd planned the whole event," he said, "and we started by asking each of the students to choose which model they wanted to work with. There were fifty students and three hairstyling classes over the course of the week. I started things off with a cutting demonstration onstage, giving a running commentary as I worked, and showing them how to do each section. As I went along, I discussed the hair – its length, texture and suitability for different treatments."

"How did the students respond?" I asked.

"To be honest with you, Jill, I was really surprised by what I found," Aitch replied. "Coming from L.A., with all its style and sophistication, I had certain preconceptions about how different it was going to be in Jamaica. But as I walked into the conference room, I instantly spotted something I hadn't expected."

I raised my eyebrows, intrigued by what Aitch was going to reveal.

"It was a stifling hot day," he continued, "over forty degrees, and so all the women had slipped off their shoes as they sat waiting for me. The first thing I noticed was that every single one of them had the most beautifully painted toenails in different shades. I had no idea that pedicures and manicures of that quality and finish were available on the island, but it instantly told me that these were the kind of women I could work with," he laughed.

"I knew that the students all ran their own salons on the island, but I soon realised that the masterclass was a really big thing for them," Aitch said. "A creative director from Vidal Sassoon had come to Jamaica from L.A., and they knew this was a fantastic opportunity to learn, but we had to improvise quite a bit in how we set things up."

"In what way?" I asked.

"Well, the models would normally have been provided with a wardrobe of suitable outfits," Aitch said, "but in Jamaica that wasn't possible, so I had to make do with what we had. We agreed that the models would wear cutting gowns, but I asked them specifically to wear their own shoes and gloves to make their own personal statement. I have to say they looked surprisingly glamorous, and I could tell from their big smiles that they enjoyed every minute of it. Of course, it was a completely new experience for the students to see a male hairdresser in Jamaica, but these women were determined to make the most of the training, and they warmed to me as much as I warmed to them. As a bunch of entrepreneurs, they were a real tour de force, and I took a lot of personal satisfaction from working with them.

"From the outset," he continued, "I decided the training shouldn't be strictly textbook. It needed to be more intuitive and organic. For me, it was just like going back to the early doctrine at Vidal Sassoon. I remembered how we'd worked with models in demonstrations back then. I was using my eye a lot – turning the model's head to see different angles, showing discipline in my sectioning, and not starting in the same place each time. I wanted to show how that helps to develop technique and individual cutting style.

"At the beginning, I had to assess each student's ability. As I expected, every one of them had a slightly different aptitude, but I didn't want anyone to feel inferior. I watched very carefully the way they handled the scissors, the comb and the hairdryer to identify any awkwardness in how they held the equipment. I observed how they combed their own hair, and from all those observations I made decisions about how to bring out the best in them.

"You see, Jill, some students start out determined to be cutters, but then you discover that they're much better at colouring hair. So you have to be able to observe and guide students into their areas of natural ability, whatever their personal preferences might be.

"There was a conference room at the hotel set aside for us for the preparation and the one-on-one classes, but it was also part of the programme that I would do some of the demonstrations on a stage in the open air," Aitch said. "It was really really hot and at first I felt quite intimidated being watched by so many people. I also found it difficult to project my voice as it was outdoors, but everyone was really excited about what was going on, and that for me was empowering."

"As you'd expect, Jill," Aitch said, with one of his knowing smiles, "I'd brought a vast wardrobe with me – a different outfit for each session and eventuality. I needed to project a professional image and what I wore was all part of that. For the showcase demonstrations, I wore a lightweight black and white houndstooth suit. It had a cropped jacket, matador style, with a nehru collar, and I wore a black silk Yves St Laurent shirt that had delicate mother of pearl buttons down the front. My trousers were high waisted, and I finished the look with my favourite Hermès belt. I felt very comfortable in how I looked, and that gave me the inner confidence I needed as I went out to strut my stuff on stage.

"We organised subtle mood music to play in the background to create atmosphere despite the vastness of the al fresco setting and the highly choreographed nature of the show. The models all had wonderfully chiselled looks, and between them they had a full range of hair textures and different skin tones from the lightest to the warmest – that gave me a lot of scope to showcase different techniques. I found ways of making the models look larger than life by encouraging them to exaggerate their poses, and I taught them how to take their time on the catwalk, and how to pause for applause. There was a huge amount of gaiety amongst the young girls as they got dressed and made up, and I was touched to see the harmony and pleasure the whole experience was clearly giving them.

"At the end of the course, each of the students received a certificate from the Vidal Sassoon Academy, which they took back to display in their salons. I stood clapping each one of them at the graduation ceremony with a real sense of professional and personal pride. Then, much to my surprise, the President of Richardson-Vicks who'd turned up for the show walked forward and presented me with an award for outstanding creativity. As we shook hands, he told me I was one of the best teachers he'd ever met. That meant a huge amount to me, and it still does." For a second Aitch looked a little self-conscious before adding coquettishly, "But maybe Jill he just fancied me!"

We both roared with laughter but despite Aitch's deliberate attempt to add fun and flirtation to the situation I could tell how significant this experience had been for him. It had clearly been a career highlight and a triumph of his skills and expertise overcoming his inner anxieties. It also demonstrated what a natural and gifted teacher he was; he knew how to nurture talent and he motivated his students whatever their abilities.

My time at the salon was up, but I was already feeling a whole lot better than when I'd arrived. As Aitch brushed me down, took my gown and held my coat for me, I could see that there was one more thing he wanted to say. "My tools and skills have always been my defence," he whispered in my ear. It was a profound statement, but I didn't have time to respond as I picked up my things and walked out of the salon.

As I made my way back to the office, I couldn't get Aitch's words out of my head. He'd summed up so much in a short phrase. His professional success was founded on learning his craft and applying it with the skill of an artisan. It seemed to me there was something universal in the way professionals relied on their technical skills, craftsmanship and professionalism to conquer their fears.

There are, of course, extraordinary ways of setting hearts alight, but the ordinary and teachable way is by good manners.

Villiers David,
Advice to my Godchildren

SON OF A PREACHER MAN

I'd always sensed that other women were much more comfortable than I was at the hairdressers. Over the years I'd watched and quietly envied them. They seemed to know the rules and sat down in front of the mirror confident about what they wanted and with a natural rapport with their stylist. Other women didn't come across as unsure about how to behave, or anxious about what sort of tip to give. As far as I could tell, they weren't worrying, like I invariably was, about whether they would be considered rude if they didn't engage in conversation, how it was possible to drink coffee whilst the stylist was busy cutting their hair, or whether they should take off their earrings at any point in the proceedings. I watched in awe as they sat back, read magazines and relaxed.

Then they'd start an animated conversation with their stylist, swapping news and gossip, with all the ease in the world. I had friends who talked about their hair stylist with gushing enthusiasm, who wouldn't dream of going anywhere else for their regular haircut or colour treatment. They would wait weeks to make sure they could see their personal stylist. I guess you'd describe my approach as promiscuous by comparison. I'd never had a regular stylist, and I thought nothing of visiting different salons in convenient places if I needed a haircut at short notice. I'd never been loyal to a single salon or sought out a particular stylist, and up to now that had suited me just fine.

But in no time at all, it seemed I'd gained a new sense of ease in the hairdressing salon. Thanks to Aitch, it was a place I now looked forward to entering. In part, of course, that was due to wanting to hear more of Aitch's stories, but I also realised that I could learn a lot from an occupation I'd previously dismissed as superficial and frivolous. As I sat back with my glass of water in my hand and my towel around my head, I was so much more conscious of my surroundings. Rather than keeping my head down in my BlackBerry messages, I now keenly surveyed the scene in the mirror, and watched both hairstylists and clients as they went about their business.

After a few minutes, I noticed a woman police officer come into reception. There were a lot of police about at the time as the salon was just around the corner from St Paul's cathedral, where the Occupy demonstrators were camping out. I assumed she'd popped in to check that everything was fine, so I couldn't have been more surprised when she took off her bulletproof vest, put her walkie-talkie on the shelf and sat down. From where I was sitting, I could see her big rubber soled boots under the table in front of her, and if I wasn't mistaken, she had a gun holster around her waist.

Once I'd overcome my initial surprise, it struck me that the hairdressing salon was a great leveller. We all look pretty vulnerable with our hair wet and a cutting gown around our necks. We're somehow stripped of the barriers to intimacy, and expectant that we will leave feeling better than when we came in. *Was it this sense of being laid bare that allowed such intimate conversations to take place between relative strangers?* I wondered.

Just then, Aitch arrived and we kissed each other on both cheeks. I always loved this part of the experience. Not just because of Aitch's gorgeous smell, or because of the soft embrace from his cashmere pullover, but because of the way it relaxed me and created the conditions for our next revelatory conversation. I was curious to know more about Aitch's life in Los Angeles, and why he'd finally decided to come back to the UK. By now, I felt bold enough to ask him exactly what I wanted to know.

"So, did you have a serious boyfriend when you were out in L.A.?" I asked, with the mischievous smile all mine for once.

Aitch looked a little coy, and then he began. "For sure," he said, "in fact, it started not long after I arrived there. I was staying at the Mondrian Hotel in West Hollywood at the time. It was a luxury hotel on Sunset Boulevard and a very glamorous address, but when I got back from work in the evenings all I wanted to do was find somewhere to dance. I tried out lots of different places, but when I lost my passport I couldn't get into the mainstream clubs as I didn't have the right ID. So one night I ended up going to a club in, let's just say, the wrong part of town."

It sounded deliciously intriguing. "Tell me more," I said excitedly. "What happened?"

"It was there that I met the guy who became my partner for nearly ten years – Kenneth Ryedale McMillan," Aitch continued.

"What a great name," I said, and Aitch smiled in appreciation of my comment.

"Yes, a great name, Jill, and a gentle giant of a man. Ken had only moved to L.A. a few months before I met him," he went on, "and I can still picture him in that club. He had big bright wide eyes and very white teeth. I had a really good feeling about him from the moment I first saw him. I was pretty laced with J&B whiskey by then, and my confidence was high that I was going to pull that night."

Aitch looked at me almost innocently as he flicked my fringe with his fingers before continuing, "Ken was leaning against a jukebox and I decided to hit on him, so I strode across the dance floor like a true hunter in a very upfront American sort of way. I flattered him to the full – in da hood, we'd call it 'cherpsing' – but Ken was having none of it, and despite all my flattery, he refused to come back to my place that night."

I watched Aitch in the mirror and as he spoke, I saw another side of the man I knew as my debonair hairdresser. Some of the places he frequented were a million miles from the chic salons of Beverly Hills, Chelsea or even the City of London. It felt like a glimpse into an edgier world, where a different kind of language was used, and more dangerous behaviour took place. There was little time for me to reflect further, however, as Aitch continued telling me about meeting Ken. I didn't want to miss anything.

"As you might imagine, Jill," he said, "Ken was intrigued by my English accent, and he was also very taken with my look. When I was in London, my style was influenced by *The Face* magazine, but when I moved to L.A. I adapted it. I grew my hair longer and wore black clothes with an abundance of Butler and Wilson jewellery – I'd put on loads of necklaces and tons of silver bracelets, and I could tell as soon as I walked into a room that all eyes were on me. I made a statement, and Ken and I both knew it. He was totally fascinated by me, but initially he was a bit intimidated by it all as well.

"So in the end, on that first night we reached a compromise and ended up in a Mexican burger joint." Then Aitch started to laugh, "To be honest, Jill, I think at the time I might have misheard the bit about 'joint' and hoped that something else was on offer. But we started to get to know each other; little realising that having a burger together would become one of our favourite routines after our all-night dancing sessions. Before we parted that night, we arranged to have dinner together, and after that we started to visit each other's homes and found our feelings for each other growing."

"So how come he was in that club in the first place?" I asked.

"Well," Aitch replied, "Ken was from Chicago, where being gay wasn't something to shout about at the time. His father was actually the local preacher, so he'd spent most of his life hearing about the sins of homosexuality in church. In the end, he'd come to Los Angeles to escape all that; to be the person he knew he really was. Looking back, I think I was a real revelation to him. I was English, of course, which immediately set me apart as different, but more importantly I was also comfortable with my sexuality and I was confident about who I was."

"Tell me more about your life together," I urged, keen to know more.

"Ken and I moved into the most fantastic apartment," Aitch said. "It was on the ninth floor and you could see the Hollywood sign on the mountainside out of our bedroom window. The apartment had two bedrooms, two bathrooms and oh...," Aitch sighed, rolling his eyes with deliberate dramatic effect, "... my very first walk-in closet." It was a typically Aitch moment, playful and funny.

"I felt at home at last," Aitch continued, "and Ken and I developed a strong loving relationship with a deep level of commitment and a wonderful social life. We used to go to the theatre and to the movies all the time. We went to see as many of the big stars of the day as we could – Tina Turner, Luther Vandross, Ella Fitzgerald and, of course, George Michael. An outing to the Hollywood Bowl became a big favourite of ours but we always used to buy three tickets when we went there," he said, pausing with that mischievous smile of his that I was now so familiar with.

"Why three tickets?" I asked, knowing this was just the question he was waiting for. "Well the seats were really quite small, Jill," he said, "and our picnics were always the very best, so the third ticket was for the picnic hamper."

Aitch put his scissors down and excused himself for a second. I sat giggling quietly to myself: *how preposterous, but how very like Aitch to give the picnic basket the same status as a fellow concertgoer.*

Aitch returned and put his hands on my shoulders. I sensed he wanted to revive his memories of Ken by talking about him to me.

"It was a very caring relationship," he went on, "and I was so lucky that he was passionate in his love for me. Things weren't always easy though. His mum came to stay with us once, which was a really big deal both for him and for her. The visit didn't go that well, to be honest with you. I don't think I realised the impact I can have on people at the time; how powerful my presence can be in that sort of situation. I was left with the feeling that she didn't really approve of me, but I think looking back she just wasn't ready to approve of her son's feelings and the life he'd created for himself with me.

"Ken and I were having such a wonderful time together in L.A. that we started to make plans for the future," Aitch continued. "In fact, I was even thinking of leaving Vidal Sassoon at the time. I was in demand for photographic shoots and product promotions, and I'd had lots of offers to do other things. Debbie Allen desperately wanted me to work with her in the film business, and I also considered going freelance and developing my own hair products. But in the end, all my dreams came to nothing."

Aitch stopped in his tracks and for a moment I thought he was going to cry. I felt concerned for him, but also curious to hear more of this story. He quickly composed himself and seemed to want to continue. I sat quietly as he took a deep breath and explained what had happened next.

"It all started, Jill, when I applied for an insurance policy and had to go for a full medical," he said. "I had a feeling at the back of my mind that something wasn't quite right, but I chose to ignore it and carried on regardless. Then I got to the point when I needed to apply for a green card to stay in the US. I was really quite naïve about the whole thing. I just assumed there wouldn't be a problem; after all I had a successful career, a property and a loving relationship, and I mixed in all the best circles in Beverly Hills – I even had clients who worked at the White House for God's sake. Some of them knew about my application and explained that there were changes to the immigration rules. They asked me if I needed a letter of introduction or anything, and made me aware that there were now mandatory medical tests involved. But I felt I could get it all sorted out myself, so I didn't take up any of their kind offers of help. Given what happened later on I wish I had done, but I just didn't think it was necessary at the time. Instead, I flew back to London with all my paperwork and went to the American Embassy to secure my green card."

Aitch stopped cutting my hair in mid-flow, and looked at me seriously in the mirror as he spoke. "I guess the first time I realised there might be something seriously wrong was when I was the last of the waiting applicants to be called," he said. "Not only that, but I was asked to go into a separate room."

"Whatever was the matter?" I asked in all innocence.

"Well, Jill," he said, with a tinge of sadness in his voice, "it turned out that my medical report showed some discrepancy in my blood tests. The results were inconclusive, but I soon realised there was no way I was going to get my green card. It was some months later during one of my regular health checks that I discovered I was HIV positive."

I could tell that Aitch was struggling to control his emotions. The story had brought back a really difficult time, a turning point in his life, which still hurt him to recall.

"I flew back to the States straight away as I didn't want to find that I couldn't even get back into the country," Aitch continued. "I wanted to say my goodbyes properly and pack up my home and my life to return to the UK."

"Was there really no alternative?" I asked.

"At some level of consciousness," Aitch said, "I guess I knew I could have just gone underground like so many other people did, and stayed in the US on an unofficial basis. But that would have meant never leaving the country, or seeing my family again, and I wasn't prepared to do that."

"So, I decided to throw a party," Aitch said, as he picked up his scissors and starting cutting my hair again. "It was a way of creating something positive out of a terribly sad situation, and it gave me pleasure and some relief from all the hard work of getting organised to come back here. We held the party at our apartment and it was, as you'd expect, an extremely smart affair," he said, looking at me over his glasses.

"I insisted on black tie, of course, and ordered the most delicious Cajun food. We served champagne with the best quality cashew nuts to everyone on arrival, and as they left I gave each of my guests a single rose to remember me by. There was a certain romance and excitement to the whole occasion despite the circumstances."

I was reeling from what Aitch had just told me, but I was reminded of the party he'd held in London when he was stressed about moving out to L.A. Here again, in the face of such devastating news, and with all its consequences, Aitch's immediate thought was to throw a party. He wanted to exit gracefully, and to say his goodbyes with style and sincerity despite feeling so upset about leaving L.A., Ken and everything he'd worked so hard for.

"It must have been a terrible time for you," I said sympathetically.

"For sure," said Aitch. "I was distraught. I had to give up a lifestyle I adored, and I had to leave behind the man I adored too. It all seemed so unfair and I was pretty bitter about it all. It was 1992 when I came back and London seemed very grey and dreary compared with L.A. As I'd been away for ten years by then, I'd also lost most of my contacts and my clients had naturally moved on to other stylists. So for a time, I was pretty miserable.

"The only thing that kept me going was the fact I'd persuaded Ken to come over and stay with me for a while; that and the fact that my mother was finally retiring from work and a very big party was arranged for her by her company with all the family and friends and colleagues invited – it wasn't to be missed. It was going to be his first ever trip to England and we were both excited about it, and about seeing each other again."

"I'm so pleased," I said, genuinely relieved that there had been something for Aitch to look forward to.

"Actually, it nearly all went wrong," he continued. "Ken was really excited about his first trip to England, and we were both so excited about seeing each other again, and then a couple of months after my return, and just as I was learning to readjust to my new life, I was invited to join the first leg of the Vidal Sassoon 50th anniversary tour to Paris. The tour started in London and there was a planned programme of visits to other cities around the world to celebrate Vidal's fifty years in the industry, all sponsored by Richardson-Vicks. It was then that I discovered to my horror that the tour dates clashed with Ken's trip to London. I felt really torn; I was desperate to see Ken again, and didn't want to disappoint him over his first trip to London. But it was a huge honour to be invited on the Paris trip, and I didn't want to let Vidal down either."

"Oh my God," I said. "What did you do?"

"I summoned up my courage," Aitch replied, "and I asked the company if Ken could accompany me on the tour. Thankfully, they said yes, so Ken ended up coming over to Paris with me – with all the models in tow."

Aitch was smiling now and well into his stride. I could tell there were more interesting stories to come. "The idea was to recreate the iconic Vidal Sassoon haircuts at the Pierre Cardin museum in the Boulevard Victor Hugo," he said. "It's an amazing glassed roof building full of mannequins displaying the best of Cardin's avant garde couture. My job was to prepare the models, and take them along to the museum where Vidal would be waiting to be interviewed by all the top journalists in the city. It was a very tight schedule and Vidal was staying at The Ritz while Ken and I were in another hotel on the other side of town.

"On the big day, I had to arrive with four models all ready to be photographed before nine o'clock. As we were leaving our hotel very early in the morning, it started to drizzle with rain. We took a taxi but the models' hair still got sprinkled with rain and they didn't look as pristine as they should have done for the press conference. Vidal was furious and insisted from then on that I stayed at the same hotel as him. And that," Aitch exclaimed, "is how Ken and I ended up staying in one of the best suites at The Ritz hotel."

"That's amazing," I said, marvelling at the fact that Aitch had not only stayed at The Ritz in Paris, but had stayed in a suite there.

As if reading my mind, he explained, "After Vidal decided we had to stay at the same hotel as him, it turned out there were no rooms available except for this one suite. It was absolutely enormous with two huge baths and a massive bed. I remember looking out of the window facing the Place Vendôme and watching a cavalcade of Mercedes snake up to the hotel entrance, with the soft light from the old fashioned streetlights gleaming on them. I stood transfixed as I watched the glamorous guests emerge and walk into the foyer – it was a scene of pure elegance.

"That evening, Vidal had a dinner in a private room at the hotel," Aitch went on, "and he invited Ken and I to join him and his family. It was a really great privilege and it showed how much respect Vidal had for me. Suddenly things in my life had started to look up again."

It was time for me to go and I snapped out of my reverie as Aitch took my gown. As I looked at my reflection, I saw how my image was subtly changing. My hair was shorter and had a jauntier look to it than the very conservative cut I'd had not so long ago. Without me realising it, Aitch was influencing my hairstyle as he told me his stories. I was learning more and more about him and his craft as a stylist, but I was also coming out of my own professional shell and showing more of my personality through my haircut.

Where would it all end? I wondered as I hurriedly grabbed my coat, paid my dues and left to go back to the office.

Grant me the serenity to accept the things I cannot change; courage to change the things I can; and wisdom to know the difference.

The serenity prayer

IN THE PSYCHIATRIST'S CHAIR

As I walked from the tube station to the salon, certain thoughts were circling round my mind as they'd been doing for some weeks now. I was at a career crossroads and felt quite confused. I was contemplating doing something completely different after over thirty years of a successful career in the City. I always knew I wouldn't want to continue forever, but it was proving hard to let go and plan for a new future. There were very few people I could confide in. My team relied on me and I didn't want to unsettle them unnecessarily, and I didn't want to show my hand to my colleagues until I'd worked out my exit plan. I was in a period of transition, but my thoughts were becoming clearer and I was determined to swap the job with so much travel, time away from home and relentless meetings, for a more creative lifestyle.

As I sat in front of the mirror, I dared to let Aitch know what was going on in my mind.

"I want to write," I said, surprising myself with the boldness of the statement. Aitch looked up and gave me his full attention. I continued a little breathlessly, hardly daring to look at him given the significance of what I was at last saying out loud. "I always have done and I don't want to leave it too late and regret not having tried," I said. "I'm going to resign and embark on a completely new phase in my life."

All of a sudden, my thoughts were spilling out and I realised – as soon as I found the courage to look in the mirror – that I was turning a subtle shade of pink.

As I'd hoped and expected, Aitch was both interested and

sympathetic. He listened carefully as I spoke while wielding his scissors with his usual aplomb. I was speaking in a kind of whisper as if afraid of making my plans a reality simply by talking about them, and it seemed strange that I was confiding in Aitch of all people. If you'd told me six months before that my hair stylist would be one of the first to hear my innermost thoughts, I'd have laughed at the very thought. But here I was, and it was strangely liberating, as if I'd unburdened myself of a huge secret.

There was a short silence before I asked, "Do many of your clients talk to you about their problems and big decisions, Aitch?" I was desperately hoping that I wasn't the only one to have embarrassed myself in this way.

"For sure," he replied, to my relief, "once we've developed a trusting relationship a lot of my clients talk to me just like this. It's safe here and I'm a great believer in talking things through. It really helps; everyone needs to belch out what's eating them up."

I winced a little at his expression, but his insights were always interesting and I wanted to hear his perspective. "Go on," I said.

"Being introverted and insular doesn't help at all," he continued. "I've learnt that myself the hard way."

"What do you mean?" I asked.

"Well, since I've been going to support meetings for people in relationships with addicts, I've had the opportunity to explore my relationships, to understand what attracts me to certain people, and I'm learning how to develop tools to help me deal with manipulative behaviour. I've realised that most of my close relationships have involved men with some sort of fragility about them. It's not obvious at first, but I soon find out that, despite the outer confidence they initially show, it's me who'll end up being the stronger one once their issues and addictions emerge."

I swallowed hard, realising that Aitch was disclosing his own private thoughts and feelings in order to demonstrate the therapeutic effect of talking things through.

"I'm sometimes asked if I've ever paid or been paid for sex," Aitch said, looking at me seriously over the rim of his designer glasses, "and in some ways I guess I have, when you look back at how things used to be.

"If you accept hospitality to go to dinner or to a concert or the theatre with someone, favours are expected at the end of the evening. I've learnt that addicts can be selfish, and there have been times when I've paid for taxis and theatre tickets and dinner, and sadly not all my friends have been able to reciprocate. I haven't always dealt with that well at the time, but now I'm able to look back and see the fun side.

"And I'm learning how to empower myself by talking to others with similar experiences. Many of them have far bigger problems than mine to deal with, and that helps to put things in perspective. It encourages me to be positive and to count my blessings. I've learnt to accept now that I'm destined to be an enabler. I need to embrace that instead of fighting it, but I also need to find ways of protecting myself and channelling my emotions into my creativity. I get great support at work and I find it particularly rewarding when my clients and colleagues take an interest in my art. They want to talk to me about it and that inspires me to focus on producing my next piece, even when there's chaos around me at home."

"When I look back over my relationships," said Aitch, "I can see how I'm somehow attracted to a certain type of guy. They've all had their demons of one kind or another. Ken, of course, had issues about being gay coming from a deeply religious family, and he found it hard to express his sexuality and his real feelings for a long time. I was the strong one who helped him find himself and to embrace who he really was.

"Before Ken, I had a long relationship with a guy called Angus and we really were a great couple for a while. Angus was well educated, he'd studied medicine at University in Canada, and he had a cut glass English accent and a wicked vocabulary. He was also most handsome and a bit of a playboy, like Ben in many ways, but by the time I met Angus I was much more mature and confident so it was more of a relationship of equals, with love, kindness and great passion."

"We had a great social life together and bought a lovely house in Carshalton that I took great delight in furnishing. It was my first real opportunity to design a home together with Angus, and it was the start of my passion for interiors. We co-ordinated everything in pink and grey with purples and lilacs. The kitchen was high gloss patent, in a deep aubergine colour, and in our bedroom we had a white carpet and, I remember, a beautiful bespoke mirrored chest of drawers with glass handles and decorated with Bristol blue medicine bottles. Our place was quite the thing back then," Aitch said, and I didn't doubt it for a second.

"Angus loved me deeply and my family absolutely adored him," Aitch continued. "He worked in the wine business so we always had a fabulous collection of exciting vintages. He came from a wealthy family in the Caribbean and he certainly knew how to spend money, not just on fine wines but on sustaining a certain lifestyle.

"What I didn't realise at the start however, although it became glaringly obvious later on, was that Angus was addicted to cocaine. As time went by, he was doing more and more coke and it was becoming a real problem. I didn't really understand what was going on as coke has never been my thing – my vice of choice has always been smoking a spliff with a glass of champagne while soaking in a huge bubble bath and eating delicious chocolates," Aitch smiled, and I smiled back.

"As I said, Angus and I had a great lifestyle," Aitch continued, "and we became firm friends with the couple who'd helped us design our home. Then it transpired they also had a cocaine habit, and as their addiction got the better of them, we drifted apart. By that time, Angus and I had been together for almost nine years. We were making plans to buy a home in Maida Vale and thought we might start building up a small property portfolio, but Angus was struggling with his addiction and it affected our relationship badly.

"I guess our relationship was another example of my fascination with the darker shades of addition. I recognise that now, but at the time it was really painful, especially when we broke up. I guess you'd say it was the first real divorce I went through. We sold the house, split the proceeds, and I reinvested in a two bedroom flat on the fashionable side of Kings Avenue in Clapham."

There was a pause while Aitch gathered himself together before continuing. "This was my blue period, Jill," he said, with his signature smile. "The interiors in my new flat were all cornflower blue in really pretty tones. I bought my first Bang and Olufsen stereo while I was there, I remember, and I treated myself to the most amazing mirrored wardrobes. I was single again, of course, and this became quite an adventurous time in my life. I tried lots of new and different things before I went out to Los Angeles."

At that moment, Aitch was called away to greet a client who'd just arrived and I sat back in the chair with some relief. This was confessional stuff, and I was nervous about what might come out next, and whether our conversation was being overheard.

"I don't know what it is about religion," Aitch said on his return, "but I have a tendency to meet guys with some sort of religious background or history. I remember a time when I met up with a guy at a club in Vauxhall and when I went back to his place I was faced with images of the Virgin and child all over the walls and masses of crucifixes everywhere. And there was another occasion when I'd gone back to a guy's house who lived near St Paul's and who kept a coffin in his home. Why am I attracted to such interesting people Jill?" Aitch asked rhetorically, as I struggled to think of a suitable answer. "A while ago," he continued, "I even went out with a priest – Pastor Darrington as he was known. He was a young guy who wore a dog collar, and was attracted to both men and women; in fact, he'd fathered two children, but somehow or other we ended up not in a relationship exactly, but seeing each other casually, so as not to compromise his street cred. He was a real hustler and looked more like a rap singer than a priest with his leather jacket and shiny gold tooth."

I was listening attentively, but as I looked in the mirror I was conscious of a stunned expression on my face with these latest revelations. I looked down to avoid Aitch's gaze for a few moments as he continued talking.

"Eventually Pastor Darrington fell from grace," Aitch said. "He left the church and started taking crack cocaine. At first, the effects were all pretty subtle, but I've learnt that that's the thing with addicts: the drugs make them manipulative, full of deception and intensely selfish. Pastor Darrington and I would arrange to meet, after he'd convinced me yet again that he wasn't taking anything and hadn't been using, and then, of course, I'd discover that he had. I was pretty naïve but, if I'm honest, the gangster rap 'cherpsing' also excited me. I also realise my home had a bit of ghetto glamour that all added to the attraction. It's always been my addiction, being attracted to guys like this; I fall for it every time and they have this ability to somehow zoom in on my gullible emotions, and that plays right into their hands. But sooner or later, that awful smell of crack would return – then the whole attitude would change and aggression would start to kick in like a demon.

"There were times when the drugs had a really bad effect on Pastor Darrington's personality. He would literally change out of all recognition, and become physically and verbally abusive towards me. It would begin when I'd refuse to give him money to buy crack, and end in a vicious argument that would disturb the neighbours in the early hours. Later on, I discovered he was carrying guns and knives and sometimes he'd threaten me with them. I wished I could have had some sort of alarm that would have gone off if he tried to come into my home with a weapon."

Aitch looked at me as he held lengths of my hair to check for consistency. He seemed deep in thought and I wasn't sure how to react to such an alarming story.

"I soon learnt it wasn't worth retaliating," Aitch continued, without any prompting. "My life was worth more than the ten or twenty pounds he wanted for drugs, and I learnt the hard way that it was useless trying to challenge the rage and anger of a crack addict. But it became quite a traumatic situation for me at home. I remember sitting anxiously at the top of my stairs worrying desperately about what was going on in my flat. I knew that some of the time he would take advantage and use my home secretly to do Class A drugs, and on one occasion, unknowingly to me, he hid there from the police. I didn't know what to do, and was under great stress at the time. I had to think of myself, my family and my neighbours. It was a period of madness and had a big effect on me.

"I realise now that I should have been more guarded. I shouldn't have taken him, and everything I thought he stood for, at face value. But I find I either trust someone completely or end up questioning them all the time – and, of course, neither is good for a relationship at the end of the day. When I analyse things though, it's always me who ends up being the strong one, however difficult or dangerous the situation becomes. I'm the one who supports and cares for these guys despite their issues. I've somehow found an inner strength and that's what saves and protects me. It's my higher power, saying a prayer and lighting a candle, that sort of thing, and it's my saving grace."

"Why did it go on for so long?" I asked trying to reconcile the strong character I knew with the situation Aitch had so graphically described.

"I guess there was a toxic excitement about it all, and if I'm honest, I think I was probably in danger of getting addicted to that. But it's complicated. With addicts, it's not awful all the time, and it was only when things got hostile, and he started acting like he was deranged, that I fully appreciated what I'd gotten into. I also learnt to appreciate that there were other issues too. I wasn't the only one affected by the Pastor's addiction, and some of his problems had nothing at all to do with me. I've learnt that all sorts of things can have an effect on an addictive personality," Aitch went on.

"I see it in Donald too. He's just come out of a period of rehab," Aitch said matter-of-factly, "but it wasn't very successful, so it's quite difficult for both of us right now. That's why the support group is so helpful to me; I've found some solace going along to these meetings."

I could tell that this was important to Aitch. His relationship with Donald mattered deeply to him, but I wasn't sure how much more he wanted to talk about it, so I kept quiet. Then Aitch continued, without prompting, to tell me about how he and Donald had met.

"Donald and I first got together around eight years ago," he said. "We met on a gay internet site called Adam4Adam that had been recommended to me by a couple of friends. They could tell that I needed a special relationship in my life, someone to love, and maybe to grow old with. Don't get me wrong, Jill, I was pretty happy with my life back then. I was having lots of fun and going out with loads of different people – and sometimes there was a reason to celebrate with a champagne breakfast the next morning and sometimes there wasn't, if you get my meaning," he giggled.

"But I was excited about meeting Donald for the first time, and we quickly discovered that we were ready for a more stable relationship. We'd both had some pretty unsatisfactory encounters up to then. I'd had a couple of really disastrous experiences with guys I met on the internet," Aitch said, rolling his eyes in mock horror, "including the time when I had to call the police after a brick was thrown through my window."

"With Donald, though, there's been a great love between us from the outset", he said, leaving the story of the broken window hanging in the air, "but he still suffers from the grief of losing his twin brother, Ronald, and that, coupled with other things, has led to alcoholism. In the early days, I didn't see it – I guess, looking back, I was probably in denial about what was going on, but once I realised he had issues, I searched desperately for ways to help him. I tried hard to show him the terrible destruction he was doing to himself and to me, but it had no effect. I would call his friends who I knew were close to him to try to make him stop, but my pursuit of eradicating his drinking hasn't worked, and I have to accept it's not something I can control.

"Since we've been together, there've been some pretty traumatic situations that quite honestly I've found highly embarrassing – especially those involving my family and friends. We're now in our tenth year together, and don't get me wrong Jill, sometimes I just want to kill him for his attitude and completely intolerable behaviour, but you know what, despite all our gladiatorial fights, our love for each other has survived."

"Does he accept he has a problem?" I asked.

"Yes," Aitch replied, "Donald's a very intelligent man struggling to help everyone but himself, but the system and continuing support he needs to continue his recovery have somehow failed him. To be honest, I've been in denial about the whole situation for a long time, but since I've sorted out some support for myself, I've learnt more deeply that alcoholism is a disease that many families try to deal with for too long without help. I've also learnt that even the smallest steps to recovery deserve recognition. He's in transition right now, but because I've known him so long it's hard sometimes to believe he's really going to change. I guess I'm also a little afraid of him changing as things have been going on like this for so long now. But Donald's always shown me love and that's what's kept us together. He always says to me he's in the relationship for the long haul. There's a great deal of love that Donald has to offer underneath all the struggle – I can see and feel that – and that's what I hold on to with hope."

There was a pause while we both took in what Aitch had been

talking about. We'd touched on some really personal issues, but as always with Aitch, there was honesty, and often a little naivety, in the way he told even the darkest of stories that made you warm to him. In that moment, the salon had a sense of real intimacy about it; a place for talking things through, a refuge where stylists and clients revealed things to each other that they'd hesitate to mention to anyone else, even to the people closest to them. Finally I'd experienced that trusted exchange of feelings with my own hair stylist that had eluded me for so long.

I didn't know what to say next. It didn't seem right to move on to holiday plans or the weather, and there was still something much more important on my mind.

"I'd love to write your story," I blurted out, somewhat to my own surprise. It'd just come to me. I wanted to be a writer. What better story to tell than his.

Aitch grinned. "For sure," he said, "that would be great."

I gathered up my belongings and walked out of the salon deep in thought. It'd certainly been an interesting conversation, full of revelations and self-analysis, and it felt curiously liberating. *Had I just come up with my game plan? Was I really serious about writing Aitch's story, and was he just being polite in his response? Only time would tell.*

Do not be self-conscious. It is better to be affected. For affectation provokes indignation or amusement, which is a compliment; whilst self-consciousness provokes pity, which is not.

Villiers David,
        Advice to my Godchildren

DECADENCE, SLEAZE AND EXCESS

"As I grow older, I want to become an accomplished dandy," said Aitch with a flourish, as his scissors skimmed over my hair with ease. "But hopefully without people thinking that I'm mad, just highly eccentric" he added, looking at me over the rim of his glasses in the mirror with a whimsical smile.

I laughed at this latest announcement and knew that yet again we were going to have a great conversation. It had all started when I complimented Aitch on how he looked when I greeted him with a kiss on the cheek.

"You look fabulous today," I'd said, looking him up and down.

"Thank you, Jill," he'd replied, with a knowing grin, well aware of the impact he'd made. On this particular occasion, he was wearing a tailored pin-stripe jacket with black and white dogtooth tweed on the collar, pockets and cuffs. "My tailor Ali from Perfect Cleaners put this together for me, but you should have seen me yesterday," he said laughing uproariously. "I was very ghetto bling. I was wearing a jacket embellished with leopard skin and sequins. It's all the rage right now, and I get regularly get comments from complete strangers in the street about how great I look."

I raised my eyebrows at the expression, and at the thought that Aitch has his own personal tailor, but I was curious to understand Aitch's statement about becoming a dandy.

"What do you mean by a dandy?" I asked, knowing full well that Aitch would be delighted to tell me.

"Well", he replied, "being a dandy is all about making a visual impact – at a time of maturity. You really can't be a dandy too early in life".

I sniggered as I thought back to all the stories Aitch had told me of his past. It seemed to me that he'd made an impact from a pretty young age.

"You see, Jill", he continued, "You have to be mature enough to have the style necessary to be a serious dandy. It's a question of practising and building confidence during your younger days, so you can be fully flamboyant at an age when it matters.

"One of my neighbours in Harlesden, for instance, is in his mid-80s, but he insists on wearing different colour shoes and socks, and I swear I saw him in the street the other day dressed in a tutu, jeans and combat boots with high heels. He's very colourful, he acts as if he's almost possessed and he's got completely mad hair. But somehow he gets away with it, and I have to admit I admire the freedom of expression he has at his age."

"Surely you wouldn't want to look like that?" I asked, slightly bemused at the image he'd described. Aitch dressed with the utmost confidence, but his distinctive style was all about tailored jackets, vivid colours and the best quality fabrics, rather than outrageous outfits and mismatching accessories. I couldn't see him in a tutu somehow, however much I tried.

"No, for sure," Aitch said reassuringly, "my dandy look would be more gangster chic with bling or tailored tweed, brogues, cashmere sweaters, frivolous cravats and, of course, pochettes."

I smiled and looked at Aitch in the mirror. He'd just described the way I'd imagined Ben had dressed, and I wondered whether he realised that. Before I could ask him, he continued in full flow.

"I get noticed a lot, Jill," he said, "and I think that's down to my inner confidence. For me, presentation is so so important. I always make sure that my shirts are immaculately laundered and my shoes are polished until they shine. In bad weather, I won't wear my shoes to work; I carry them in a shoe-bag to keep them pristine and avoid ruining them in the rain. It's really important to look after your clothes and to pay attention to every detail. I'm a stickler, for instance, for using shoetrees to keep my leather shoes in perfect shape. For years when I was travelling, I used to lug those really heavy wooden ones around in my luggage. I wouldn't go anywhere without them. Later on, I discovered plastic shoetrees. Once I started taking those away with me, I saved a fortune in excess luggage charges, I can tell you!"

"Where does your passion for clothes come from, do you think?" I asked.

"I guess it all started with my grandmother," Aitch replied. "As a seamstress she was surrounded by different fabrics, and that was the world I grew up in. It was from her that I developed a strong belief in the power of fashion to make someone look good and feel confident. My mother too always makes an effort to be well dressed, even now in her '80s. In her younger days, no one would've guessed she'd got no money; she had a way of making the most of the little she had. She's always had a wardrobe that allows her to hold her head high."

I could see how that belief manifested itself in Aitch too. He always looked expensive. He had a knack of combining a few choice pieces with accessories that made you think he did all his shopping in the chicest boutiques.

"It was from Ben that I learnt all you really need is a good quality base wardrobe," Aitch continued, – "a classic black suit with a sharp jacket, a tailored white shirt, a pair of well-fitting jeans, a raincoat and a good pair of leather shoes; and it was from Ben that I learnt the trick of putting ball bearings in the hems of my trousers to make them hang beautifully. With a quality base wardrobe, you can add all sorts of accessories such as cuff links, buttons, socks and scarves, creating a wide variety of looks and giving a sense of colour and personality to each outfit.

"I think socks and shoes are especially important," he went on. "I first discovered the joy of fine hosiery when I was in Los Angeles, and my passion for socks hasn't diminished since those days. At one time, I bought all my socks from Fougard, but I've got a much bigger collection now, from all the best menswear shops. To complement my collection of fabulous socks, I also collect shoes, which I adore – I firmly believe that anything is possible in good shoes, Jill."

I laughed and instinctively looked down at Aitch's feet. He was wearing shiny black leather brogues finished off with bright purple laces. Aitch saw me look down and said proudly, "Those laces were bought for me by one of my clients.

"There was a time in my life when I would buy a pair of Gucci shoes every season," he went on, "but right now Jeffery West is my favourite designer. I'm wearing my black pair today and I'm desperate to get a pair in tan as well, but they're not cheap. I've also got a pair of Versace black velvet ankle boots with a fabulous jewelled buckle and they look great with my black jeans and black crepe jacket with velvet collar."

I'd always thought it was women who had such passion for shoes, but Aitch was opening my eyes to how men could also have very particular tastes and desires for the latest fashions.

"Which other designers do you admire?" I asked.

"Oh that's easy," Aitch replied. "It would have to be Berluti. They make fine Italian shoes, with beautiful finishes in the softest leather you can imagine and in every exotic and subtle colour you can think of. One day, I'd love to own a pair in every single shade, particularly the one they call caviar."

Aitch paused as he examined my hair and judged what needed to be done next. There was no denying that my hair was shorter than I'd ever had it before. I'd had lots of compliments as the style had slowly become a little edgier, and quite a few people had said it made me look much younger, so I was really pleased about that. I could see that Aitch was still thinking about my question on his influences.

"A lot of it was also down to travelling around the world with Vidal," Aitch continued. "He was always really well presented and was obviously a great influence on me. I can still remember the crisp white suit he wore with a simple yellow tie when we went to the Philippines together, and the impact it made. Of course, he had a rather bigger budget than me, Jill, but I learnt from him that looking smart was really important.

"On that particular trip, we were invited to a gala evening organised to showcase the creativity of the Philippines. We went to see a Filipino designer – Vidal, me and the crew – who measured us all up and made each of us a personal barong to wear for the occasion."

Aitch saw the puzzled look on my face and quickly explained. "A barong is a big white shirt," he said. "It's the national formal wear for men and it has a thin collar, French double cuffs and a vent on each side. It's made of a sheer material that's quite transparent – quite frankly you need a good body to show off underneath it. It's at times like that when all the working out in the gym pays off," he said, giggling a little at his own hubris.

"We wore our barongs with smart black evening trousers and stood in line at the front of the stage as we were presented with bouquets of cascading tropical flowers. I have to say we did look gorgeous."

I smiled as Aitch beamed at me in the mirror. Somehow he managed to get away with outrageous statements like this with a disarming combination of chutzpah and charm.

Aitch used his fingers to check that the length of my hair was consistent. I was about to ask him more about his love of clothes when he spotted someone arriving at the salon and excused himself for a moment. I watched in the mirror as he glided across the floor, and went up to her.

"Alright, girlfriend?" he said, with one of his biggest grins, before giving the young woman affectionate kisses on both cheeks. It was quite obvious they knew each other well, and just for a second, I saw Aitch's salon persona slip effortlessly into a slightly less poised version of himself. For once, he wasn't performing for a client, he was being himself and he was hip. They stood in animated conversation for a few minutes and I busied myself checking my BlackBerry and answering a few emails.

Aitch came back smiling and apologetic for keeping me waiting. "That was one of my old colleagues," he explained, "she used to work here in the salon. She runs her own salon now, but always pops in when she's in town to say hello to me."

"Now, where were we?" he asked.

"We were talking about the influences on your wardrobe," I replied.

"Ah yes," said Aitch. "What you have to remember is that from my very early days, I was always conscious that I was representing Sassoon – both the company and the man – and I wanted Vidal to feel he had a team presenting themselves in the way he'd expect. He was always really well turned out with pressed seams in his trousers and beautifully coordinated accessories. There were also all the fantastic men's designer collections we did over the years at London Fashion Week, and the degree shows at St Martin's. They were an opportunity to refine and buff up one's image, shall we say," he smiled.

"And, of course, I like to observe other guys who've adopted a unique or distinguished style of their own and I put the images of what I see in my memory bank for future reference. It might be that I fancy them too, of course," he giggled, "and if I see a guy who's really well dressed, or who's wearing a pair of shoes that take my fancy, I let him know and start cherpsing, making a move on him. It's a great form of engaging and showing love and appreciation, and Jill," he sighed, "it gives me so much pleasure to see and hear the responses I get when I flirt, not just with men but with women too."

Aitch gave me one of his glances that combined mock coyness with a glint of sinfulness. "In fact," said Aitch, "you could say that flirting was a pastime of mine – depending on how gorgeous the person is, of course."

It was true. I'd seen it for myself in the salon; the casual physical contact, the knowing looks and the sharing of small intimacies. He was an incorrigible and accomplished flirt, with clients and colleagues, men and women – with pretty much everybody really.

"Did Vidal impact your style in other ways?" I asked, keen to get back to Aitch's influences, and a little self-conscious around his overtly flirtatious behaviour.

"Well, back in the '80s," he replied, "I acquired a collection of Versace ties that Vidal always complimented me on – and that made me feel really good. I've still got those ties funnily enough, though they're considered vintage now. I like to tie them very loosely and twist them around my collar, more like a cravat than a conventional tie, and each one makes its own statement.

"There's something wonderful about cravats don't you think, Jill?" Aitch asked rhetorically. "Wearing a tie makes you look instantly smart, but wearing a cravat makes you instantly elegant." And as he was speaking, I could summon up images of the different ties and scarves I'd seen Aitch wearing in the salon – in wonderfully rich colours and tied in unusual eye-catching ways.

"Then, of course, there is my collection of handkerchiefs," Aitch continued, with a hint of something devilish to come. "I learnt about the elegance of a handkerchief in the top pocket of a jacket from observing the best dressed men during my travels – but now, of course, I understand so much more about colour coding." Aitch paused, and from his askance look I knew he had another naughty secret to share.

"What do you mean?" I asked, knowing he was dying to tell me.

"Well, Jill," he explained, "in the gay community, the colour of your handkerchief and where you wear it in your back pocket, gives out a certain message." By now, he was grinning and clearly amused by my naivety.

"What sort of message?" I asked, on cue.

"You really don't want to know," Aitch beamed, "but let's just say that it says something about your preferences."

I was amused by the notion, but grateful that Aitch knew better than to delve further into the details of colour-coded gay sexual messages right there in the salon. Then he giggled as if enjoying a private joke.

"In fact, I used to get confused at times when I was in L.A.," he said, "as the gang community also had a colour-coded system, and I had to be very careful with my colours and the placement of my handkerchiefs not to mix up my messages, if you get my meaning." With that he flounced off to the reception desk and I was left reflecting on his funny story.

"Did you pick up any influences on your travels?" I asked when he returned.

"Of course I did, Jill," he replied, as if he couldn't believe I'd asked such an obvious question. "I found inspiration in fabrics and styles from lots of different places, both for my wardrobe and for my hair designs. For instance, I went on a Sassoon Academy trip headed up by Christopher Brooker and Annie Humphries once to a Club Med resort in Senegal, and I was blown away by the colours and the textures of the fabrics there. I ended up selling the clothes I'd taken with me and using the money to barter for fabrics to bring back with me. I created quite a stir when I turned up at Heathrow in bare feet just wearing a sarong, I can tell you."

I smiled at the thought of Aitch's typical bravado as I pictured him striding out of the airport terminal wearing such a bizarre get-up and making his way home to Harlesden on the bus.

"Even the sandals everyone was wearing over there inspired me – I used the imagery it summoned up to create a gladiatorial hairstyle," Aitch said, "with local fabrics woven into the hair to give texture and structure and to allow the vivid colours and light of Africa to shine through."

I was looking at Aitch in the mirror and taking in the outfit he was wearing that day with a more educated perspective. I noticed that the double cuffs of his pristine white shirt were visible just below his sleeve revealing a pair of jet-black cufflinks. Aitch saw my eyes settle on them.

"My cufflinks always have to be stylish," he said. "I don't like jokey cufflinks, or funny socks for that matter. My clients have a certain elegance about them and I'm drawn to that. I feel I owe myself respect and, of course, I want to be a gentleman – just as I've taught myself to be."

"How long does it take you to get ready in the morning?" I asked, curious as to what it took to create the right look every day.

"Not long at all, Jill," he replied, a little to my surprise. "I take about ten minutes to choose what I'm going to wear and fifteen minutes to shave and get dressed, which means I have plenty to time to polish my shoes.

"But I have to confess," Aitch said a little conspiratorially, "I hate washing and ironing with an absolute passion. So I've decided that having my shirts laundered is one of my perks in life. I'm very particular about my shirts as you might imagine. So having them laundered means they look just so and that makes all the difference to the look. God, I've had some fabulous shirts in my time when I think back. One of the first ones I bought, which I loved to death, was a flowered shirt that came from a shop I adored on the Kings Road. I can still remember how soft it felt against my chest. It was made of sheer voile and fitted me like you'd never believe."

As Aitch spoke, he was puffing out his chest and almost recreating the look as he remembered the impact he'd had in that shirt.

"I knew I looked sexy and I made the most of it," he said, with a wicked grin. "It was a fawn colour with brown and mustard-coloured flowers all over it, and a big sloppy collar and tight sleeves. It was pretty much transparent too, so it showed off my body perfectly, and I used to wear it with hipster jeans and platform shoes – quite the '70s ghetto pimp look!" he laughed.

I sat back and smiled at the thought of Aitch prancing up and down the Kings Road and no doubt turning heads as he did so.

"I'm quite often aware of people looking at me when I walk down the street," Aitch continued. "Even now someone will call out to me as I'm walking along, 'Hello son, you're looking nice', or I see a couple looking at me and commenting to each other as I pass by. The other day I was helping a lady with her luggage on the train and she said 'Oh, you're the man with the nice necklace'. I like being noticed, Jill, it makes me feel good, and it makes all the thought and effort seem worthwhile. "

There was no doubt that Aitch was vain, but his playfulness, the way he went just a little over the top to make you laugh, somehow gave an acceptability to the brazen showmanship. My haircut was finished and as I looked in the mirror, it was obvious my own look had been subtly changing. I wondered how close I was getting to Aitch's original vision of what my hair should look like.

As I took off the nylon cutting gown, and put my Maxmara jacket back on, it struck me how I too wore a uniform and sustained a certain style with my business wardrobe. I had a range of sharp suits and dresses with jackets for work from places like L K Bennett and Austin Reed, and I carefully chose the ones I knew I looked best in for my most difficult meetings, or the days when I knew I needed to be at my most confident. But when I went home, I changed into jogging pants and a fleece, washed the make-up off my face and relaxed.

"I bet you have the most amazing casual wardrobe," I said, as I prepared to leave, conjuring up images of Aitch in the latest designer weekend wear.

To my surprise, he was quick to contradict me. "Not at all, Jill," he said. "In fact, Donald always says I'm a completely different person when I get home. I shred the salon image and de-robe, dropping each layer of my clothes onto the floor like ecclesiastical robes. Then I put on mismatching clothes and luxuriate in my own version of grunge with no tailoring or designer labels in sight. I go clubbing sometimes at the weekends, and then I like to adopt a gangster rapper look, but it doesn't always work, so I'm having a bit of a rethink about that one. Maybe I need to add a diamond in my tooth, and a gold necklace the size of an industrial toilet chain."

Aitch looked at me in the mirror with a wicked smile and quickly excused himself as his next client had just arrived. It gave me time to reflect on his final comments. They'd revealed a different side to him than the stylish fashionista I'd got to know in the salon. He'd shown a glimpse of another aspect to his personality, which was quite different from the sophisticated creature he appeared to his clients: an alternative persona who frequented a wholly different world. When he returned it was time for me to go, and as Aitch took off my cutting gown, I knew that sadly there wasn't time to explore this further.

Then, just as I turned to leave, he grinned at me and lifted up his left leg, pointing to the bottom of his black Jeffery West shoe. I didn't understand what he was doing at first, but I looked closer to where he was pointing, and there, clearly inscribed in the sole, were three words – Decadence, Sleaze and Excess. It summed it all up really; underneath that stylish designer look was pure unadulterated hedonism.

There are black people on this planet with very black skins. They are your relations. Resist everyone who tries to make you forget this.

Villiers David,
Advice to my Godchildren

EAST OF HARLESDEN

I was sitting with my hair in a turban drinking a cup of tea and thinking about my trip to Japan, when Aitch came up and put his hands on my shoulders. He gently removed the towel and ran his fingers through my hair.

"It's keeping its shape nicely, Jill," he said, "but I think we can go a little shorter this time."

We both knew what he was doing. He was pushing the boundaries towards that vision he'd had for me from the very beginning. And I was more than happy to go along with his suggestion.

"When are you off on your travels again?" he asked, always ready to show genuine interest in my next business trip.

"Funnily enough, I was just thinking about that," I replied. "I'm off to Japan next week."

"How wonderful," said Aitch, smiling at me as he combed my hair through.

"To be honest," I said, "I find Japan one of the most challenging places to visit. It's quite an impenetrable place in many ways". I was thinking back to the first time I'd arrived at Narita airport, and the anxiety I'd felt about buying the right ticket for the bus journey to get to my hotel when everything was in Japanese and it was late at night.

"I know what you mean," Aitch said. "I found it a difficult place as a black man arriving there for the first time thirty years ago."

I should have known that Aitch had been there too. "Yes, I can understand that," I said. "What were your experiences of Japan like?"

"Actually," said Aitch, "the first time I went there, I felt as though I'd always been expected."

"What do you mean?" I asked, slightly thrown by his answer.

"Well, when I was a young boy in Dominica," Aitch explained, "my grandmother gave me a series of little storybooks. The stories were in English, but all the characters were oriental. I just loved those books, especially the vivid illustrations that showed them dressed in beautiful silk kimonos carrying delicate parasols.

"Somehow I knew deep down that one day I'd travel to Asia and be among people who looked just like that. I've always had the ability to visualise something bigger, something grander," said Aitch. "Even as a young child, I somehow knew that my life was going to be so much more than living in Dominica."

It was a touching story and Aitch had one of those misty looks in his eyes that I'd learnt to recognise when he reflected on his past. But he soon became animated as he continued his story.

"From the way Japan was depicted in those story books," he said, "I'd always thought of it as being a series of charming little village communities. So you can imagine my surprise when I first arrived in Tokyo, and it turned out to be a teeming modern city, full of colour and energy and noise."

"So when were you in Tokyo?" I asked, settling back in my chair and anticipating another fascinating story.

"It all started in the '70s," he began. "Vidal had a real passion for Japan; he loved the symmetry of the architecture, and he was a great admirer of Tadao Ando, who inspired his work – just like the Bauhaus architecture.

"One of the early models that Vidal worked with was Nancy Kwan, who was actually Chinese. When he first met her, she had really long hair, but she trusted Vidal and was brave enough to let him cut it short. And that cut became known as the Kwan bob – one of the iconic styles of its time.

"As a company, Sassoon built strong links with Japan over the years, and Vidal used to support and encourage young Japanese stylists by providing scholarships for them to come over to Europe and London to work alongside Western stylists. As a result of that I got to work with a stylist called Yoko Ishii, and when my first trip to Japan was organised, she came along with me to act as my interpreter. Yoko had completed her original training in Japan and then came over to Europe and studied at the Vidal Sassoon academy in the mid '70s. Since then, she's been a pioneer in promoting and campaigning for haircutting techniques in Japan, and for many years now she's run the Sassoon global scholarship program."

"So what took you to Japan that first time?" I asked.

"Well," Aitch replied, "I was asked to go there as the lead stylist for a creative show in Tokyo, and as you might imagine, I was really excited about it. The company put me up at the Okura, which was a luxurious traditional hotel. I remember a huge Japanese lantern in the lobby. I was told it symbolised the spirit of harmony and hospitality, and I grew to understand how important that spirit is to Japanese culture while I was there.

"The hotel staff wore kimonos and I was quickly introduced to Japanese food as they only served traditional dishes there. I thought sushi was very odd back then, I can tell you Jill. I couldn't understand why anyone would want to eat cold raw fish. I did try it, but it was only years later when I was in L.A. and my friends took me to sushi bars and taught me about it properly that I came to love it like I do now."

"What about tempura? I asked. "Did you try that when you were in Japan?"

"Ah tempura," Aitch sighed, looking towards the ceiling, "I just adore it. You can cook it in so many different ways – from octopus to exotic vegetables – and I love the way the tempura is made with that special flour that keeps it really light. You know, if I was ever fortunate enough to have a grand kitchen of my own, I'd buy the very best deep fat fryer and use different flavoured oils – rosemary, garlic, even mint maybe, who knows – to cook the most delicious tempura for my guests."

I could tell that Aitch was creating his own special recipe right there in the salon, but I interrupted him to learn more about what else he'd enjoyed about Japan.

"What about sake?" I asked.

"Oh, I loved that too, Jill, from the very first time I tasted it," he replied instantly, licking his lips. "I was lucky that the PR guys, who looked after me while I was there, introduced me to all the different types and flavours of sake. I've always loved natural drinks like that. I was also taken to the early morning fish market," he continued, "where they auction the tuna, salmon and whatever's the catch of the day. It's a kind of ritual enhanced by the amazing light at that time of the morning as the sun slowly rises and Tokyo awakes.

"There were so many things I saw that I fell in love with in Japan – the charcoal prints, the cherry blossom in the spring and the wonderful shapes of the trees in snow in the winter. I adored the fine quality of the silk – so much so that I bought a pale blue silk kimono for my mum with intricate embroidery all over it. She still has it hanging in her wardrobe, would you believe. I also bought a set of fabulous playing cards for myself that have a Japanese poem on each card. They're known as a hundred poems for a hundred players and come from the traditional Ogura Hyakunin Isshu anthology. I was introduced to Kabuki on that first trip too," Aitch went on, before pausing as he realised that I was struggling to keep up.

I'd been to Japan myself a few times, and enjoyed the food, the sake and the fish market too, but Kabuki was a new one on me.

"Kabuki is a form of classical dance drama," Aitch explained. "It's famous for being highly stylised, and for the elaborate make-up worn by the performers. The other wonderful thing about Kabuki," he grinned, "is that all the parts are played by men; women are banned from performing it, so the actors are all cross-dressing men." He laughed as I looked at him quizzically, wondering whether to believe him or not.

"In fact," Aitch continued, "while we were there, we created a new haircut called the Kabuki, which was inspired by the performances we experienced. We put on this amazing show in a huge conference centre in Tokyo. The models were dressed in kimonos and arrived from different directions and angles on the escalators. It was a gorgeous sight, quite beautiful to behold, and I have to say that cutting Japanese hair was a real delight. It tends to be heavy, the sort of hair that has the ability to retain its shape and to swing beautifully. It's ideal for the Sassoon style and I found it very rewarding to work with."

"But you said it was quite difficult for you there?" I said, wondering what he'd meant by that.

"I suppose it was only when I visited Kyoto that I really appreciated how different I was to them," he said. "It's a much more traditional city than Tokyo, and the children there were constantly running up to take a closer look at me. The kids were naturally curious about my strange features, my fuller lips, frizzy hair, large eyes and of course, my black skin. But it was all rather endearing and I didn't mind it."

Aitch excused himself for a few minutes and I reflected on what it must have been like for him arriving as a black man in Tokyo all those years ago. It started me wondering whether Aitch had ever had a more hostile reception on his travels. When he returned, I asked him. From his reaction, I knew he hadn't needed any time to think about my question.

"By far the worst reaction I've ever had was in Taiwan," he said, "when I arrived in the early hours of the morning from the Philippines on the Vidal Sassoon tour of Asia."

He paused and I hesitated, unsure whether to press him further. I was keen to hear about what had happened in Taiwan, but I didn't want to miss out on his experiences in the Philippines either. I was desperately hoping that my haircut would last long enough to hear both stories.

I left a short silence to let Aitch continue in his own way. "It was in the Philippines that I had my first police escort," he said, with a note of bemused pride in his voice, and my attention was immediately hooked.

"How come?" I asked, sensing there was whole lot more he wanted to tell me.

"I was having the most luxurious time," he grinned, "staying at the famous Manila hotel which had hosted Presidents, film stars and now Aitch Peters. We were invited to the royal palace, and I was on my way there with Vidal and his wife Ronnie, to attend to the first lady Amelita Ramos. We were picked up by a stretch limo that had been arranged by Leo Burnett, the PR agency, and escorted by the police all the way there. There were presidential flags fluttering on the vehicles, which created a lot of curiosity about us, and there were people straining to get a view through the crowds that lined the streets. I felt positively regal. They'd closed the roads for our cavalcade, which was a relief as the traffic in Manila was quite treacherous.

"Of course, Jill, I was devastated that I wasn't attending to Imelda Marcos herself," he said, with mock outrage, "but sadly she'd already fallen from grace by then. Can you imagine the conversation she and I could have had about shoes. For sure girlfriend!"

My mind was full of questions. "What was it like in the palace, and how did the haircut go?" I asked.

"Well, when we got there, we were greeted by officials and escorted to a reception room in one of the wings of the palace," Aitch replied. "To be honest I was a bit underwhelmed. I suppose I'd expected to be working in a grand royal hall, but this was a more intimate state room furnished with ornate furniture and furnishings finely finished with handmade embellishments that I learnt later were a feature of traditional Philippine crafts. Sadly, there was no throne that I could perch on, but it was at least my first time in a real palace – apart from my own palace in da hood, of course," he said with a wink.

I smiled back, wondering momentarily what his place was like before I asked about the first lady.

"She was surrounded by her ladies-in-waiting," Aitch said, "but full of smiles and very welcoming. She was petite, like a tiny exotic bird, and with a kind of regal elegance. As she extended her hand to me, I remember thinking that this was the first real queen I'd ever met – quite different from the trashy ones I'd met in dark smoky bars over the years. She had a kind of ethereal reserve about her that I certainly hadn't found in any of the other old queens I'd ever met," Aitch said, putting his hands on his hips and laughing loudly.

"We were served tea from an exquisite monogrammed china tea set," he continued, "and the conversation was light and humorous. She had a natural humility that I remember thinking was quite striking for someone with such a distinguished pedigree."

I was eager to hear about the haircut itself, and Aitch sensed my impatience. "We were surrounded by the Manila press who were covering the whole event," he said. "Then Vidal made an introductory speech praising my abilities, which I found a little overwhelming and very humbling, before I got down to cutting her hair. The first lady's name was Amelita Ramos, but she was known affectionately by everyone as Ming.

"To my delight the next day, there was a photo of the first lady with her new haircut on the front page of the newspapers, and it was immediately christened the Ming cut. And that," Aitch said with a flourish, "is how the famous Ming haircut came about."

"How amazing" I said, genuinely impressed with Aitch's role in the creation of the Ming haircut that even I'd heard of. "Were you really nervous attending to Filipino royalty?" I asked.

"Yes, I was a little", he replied, "but the experience helped me a lot to learn how to deal with dignitaries. You quickly understand in a situation like that that you're not doing the haircut for your own benefit, and I learnt to put myself at a discrete and respectful distance. I stood erect in her presence and spoke only when I was spoken to – I'm sure even Villiers David would have been proud of my perfect manners," Aitch laughed.

It was touching to hear him refer again to the book that had clearly formed so much of his approach to life. Ben had taught him well.

"At the end of my time at the palace," Aitch continued, "the first lady gave me a personal gift. It was a handmade rotunda box, tightly woven with a red velvet interior and with the presidential crest and her name embossed on it. It's one of the precious mementoes I've kept. It reminds me of a very special time in my life."

"What happened next wasn't quite so good though," said Aitch, and I could tell by the seriousness of his voice that he was about to tell me about his bad experience in Taiwan.

"I was on a high after the triumph of the trip to the Philippines and the next stop on the itinerary was Taiwan," he continued. "I was travelling ahead of Vidal to set everything up for him, and at that point of the trip I was pleased that everything was going really well. It was extremely hot so I was travelling in just shorts and a tee shirt, with my Prada sunglasses perched on my head to give my look a touch of style. I'd checked in the rest of my luggage, so when I arrived at Taiwan airport in the early hours of the morning I was feeling light and carefree.

"As soon I got to the front of the immigration queue, however, things started to change dramatically. The guy on the desk kept looking at me, and then at my passport photo, with a sort of disbelieving sneer. He commented that I looked young for my age, and then before I knew what was happening, I was taken to one side and marched into a holding cell where three or four guys started barking questions at me. 'Where are you going?' 'What are you doing here?' – that sort of thing. They spoke English pretty badly, but believe me, Jill, they got their point across alright. I felt completely harassed, and the most worrying thing for me was that I had no idea why they were treating me like this.

"After a while, the Head of Customs came into the room, and I sensed that things were about to get a whole lot worse. He was a really big guy and stank of alcohol. He was also very angry in a nasty sort of way. After a lot of shouting, he put his face right up to mine and told me they were going to deport me to the Caribbean. I tried to explain that I was British and living in California, but for some reason he refused to believe me."

"After that, the guys pulled out a huge world map that was written entirely in Chinese and insisted that I showed them where I came from. By now, as you can imagine, I was really stressed out, and however hard I tried I just couldn't find my tiny island of Dominica – and that just seemed to make them even madder. The interrogation went on for hours, and I was getting more and more worried about the things I should have been doing ahead of Vidal's arrival. I couldn't imagine how I was going to get out of the situation I found myself in, and all I kept thinking about was how I was the advance party and I didn't want to let Vidal down.

"I showed them all my bankcards, credit cards, whatever I had on me, but they refused to be pacified. It was at that point that I started to understand that part of the problem was my colour. I don't imagine they'd seen many black guys before, and they certainly didn't expect someone like me to be part of any important high-profile tour. Don't get me wrong, I told them about my job with Vidal Sassoon and begged them to believe me that I was there with important work to do. But it was hopeless."

"How on earth did you manage to get away?" I asked, horrified at what I'd heard. "Well some hours later, Vidal arrived as planned on his own flight, and the customs official, thank God, asked him if he knew me. As soon as he said 'yes of course he did, I was one of his core team', I was released.

"To my shame, I burst into tears when I saw Vidal – I was just so upset that all this had happened to me, and I hadn't been able to prepare things for him as I'd planned. I was mortified both about my situation and about showing all that emotion in front of him, but Vidal was really sympathetic and understood how I was feeling – so much so that he actually arranged for me to have a week's all expenses paid vacation in Hong Kong to relax and get over the whole traumatic experience."

Aitch paused and I didn't know what to say. Recalling the experience clearly upset him even now, and I couldn't tell what hurt him more, the unfair treatment and prejudice of the customs officials, or the fact that he felt he'd let Vidal and himself down. I suspected it was the latter. Aitch never wanted to let anyone down, least of all Vidal.

"I'm determined never to go back to Taiwan in a hurry," said Aitch, smiling again at me in the mirror. "I learnt afterwards that apparently if I'd given them some money the problem might have been resolved, but at the end of the day, I knew I hadn't done anything wrong. It was only my inner strength that got me through it."

My haircut was nearly finished and it looked great. I'd grown to enjoy the final stages where I could see it in its full glory. I looked in the mirror with that smile I knew Aitch was waiting for. It struck me as extraordinary that he'd lived such a full and remarkable life. *How many of Aitch's other clients knew about the places he'd been to and the adventures he'd had?* I wondered.

Aitch brushed the hair from my shoulders and led me to the reception desk. I wanted to say something: to tell him how much I admired and respected him. But now was not the time or the place, and besides I could tell he knew that without me having to say it. As he put my coat around my shoulders, I held him tighter than usual while we said our goodbyes. As I walked out of the salon, I wondered just what our next conversation would reveal.

Express a passionate conviction of your own,
and you at once create a new world.

Villiers David,
    Advice to my Godchildren

THE ARTIST WITHIN

A s I leant my head back in the basin at the salon, I saw one of Aitch's paintings hanging proudly on the wall. He had a distinctive artistic style, using bold colours with texture and movement; the sort of paintings you saw something different in every time you looked at them. I made a mental note to ask Aitch more about his artistic inspirations and influences. He was a talented artist and I was interested in how his creativity had developed over the years.

I waited for Aitch in the cutting chair and looked at myself in the mirror. I no longer buried my head in a newspaper or attended compulsively to my BlackBerry when I was in the salon. I was confident to look at myself, and I was excited about talking to Aitch again. It had become a real highlight in my work schedule, so much more interesting than sitting in long business meetings all day. Aitch and his stories made me feel alive, and they increasingly sparked my own long buried sense of creativity.

Aitch arrived and I could hardly wait to get started. "I just love your painting," I exclaimed.

"Thank you, Jill," he said with all the quiet modesty I'd grown to expect. "That one's called Peridot. I painted it to help raise money for Eve Avis who's a colleague of mine and who was climbing Kilimanjaro for the Macmillan cancer research fund. It was my first attempt at working with just one colour – vivid shades of green."

"I'd love to know more about your art, Aitch," I blurted out, "and the influences behind your creativity".

I knew it wouldn't take much. This was a subject close to Aitch's heart, and one he was going to enjoy talking about.

"When I look back," he began, "I can see how a lot of my influences came from my grandmother. I grew up with colour, with the gentle whirring of her black Singer sewing machine, and the sound of her big industrial scissors cutting material on the wooden table in our kitchen. She was always embellishing things; adding small details to outfits and making plain things look beautiful. When I was very young, I already had a keen eye for art that grew out of those experiences, but to be honest, it took some time before I took up painting in a serious way."

"Did you study art at school?" I asked.

"Funnily enough, Jill", he replied, "when I was at school, art was one of my best subjects, but I didn't give it much credence as a profession in those days. My mum kept a lot of my early work, though, and it's still there in her spare room."

He raised his eyebrows at me as if to say 'as only a mother would'. I nodded silently in recognition.

"When I was working in the Sloane Square salon," Aitch continued, "I loved going to the art shop nearby. In those days, my passion was picture frames. I spent a lot of my time in there, picking up the frames, feeling the different shapes and textures, and buying loads of polished chrome ones which were all the fashion back then."

As if on cue, one of the colour technicians came up wanting a word with Aitch, who excused himself while they discussed colour options for his next client. "I think a deep chestnut or chocolate would be best," I heard him say.

"I'm terribly sorry," Aitch said, as he returned to cut my hair. "Where were we?"

"Tell me more about colour influences," I said.

"Well, Jill", he said, "you have to remember that my colour references really started in the punk era when colouring hair was in vogue. The different blends of colour in those days made a real statement, and there was a lot of experimentation going on. I worked with leading colourists – people like Annie Humphreys, Tony LeBeau, Tracy Hayes, Peter Dawson and Edward Daley, and all the creative heads in the various salons. I've always seen colours in different hues and tones, and I tend to describe them in those terms when working with colour technicians.

"When I'm talking about colour to my clients, however, I like to make it sound exciting to listen to. So I use descriptions that reflect the seasons and which conjure up deep colours and rich images in their minds. In the summer, it's all about sandy colours like biscuit, caramel toffee or fudge. And in the winter months, it's more about smoky charcoal, conker, or petrol – colours that have a little iridescence about them. Colour changes with the seasons, just like personalities, for the simple reason that different colours reflect the light differently.

"In the summer the light can be quite savage, while in the darker seasons hair becomes duller and skin tone becomes ashen. A lot of people suffer from the lack of light in the winter, and some of them don't even know that they do, but I can see it in their faces. I like to give them a nice glazed colour, like porcelain, which reflects different iridescent tones onto their skin. It highlights the contours of their face, and lights up their day."

Yet again, Aitch was describing things to me that were obvious once I thought about them, but they'd never occurred to me before. I'd always presumed that people had their hair coloured to be fashionable, or for reasons founded in vanity. This whole interaction between the seasons, the light and the colours, made me realise there was much more to it than that.

"I don't like to carry a colour over from one season to the next," Aitch continued. "I love that sense of anticipation; waiting for the next season's colour, making it exciting. It's an accessory," he whispered, "just like changing your lipstick colour for different occasions."

I was feeling increasingly shameful as Aitch was talking. Not only had I never had my hair coloured, but I was inclined to stick with a lipstick colour for years, just buying the same one over and over again when it ran out. No doubt Aitch had noticed this about me, but thankfully he'd never commented.

I kept my embarrassment to myself as Aitch continued.

"The launch of a new collection of cuts and colour can also be influenced by different artists," he continued, making a direct connection between hair colour and art. "For example, at the salon we once did a cubism season, and one day I'd love to do a hair collection based on the work of Tamara de Lempicka. I love the fact that she makes such a strong statement in the placement of her colours – the way she puts bold colours together, and the way they complement each other – great for hair."

I broke out into a huge smile. "I love de Lempicka's work too," I exclaimed. "I first saw her work at an exhibition at the Royal Academy a few years ago, and Mike and I have a couple of her prints at home which we adore."

I felt pleased that even if my fashion and hair colouring credentials were poor, I did at least share a taste in art with Aitch. I respected his artistic opinion, and by talking about art I was starting to understand how colour had influenced him so fundamentally.

Aitch smiled at me in recognition. "I grew up around Portobello market," he said, "and to me that place is an art gallery in itself. By walking from one end to the other, I can bank a whole load of images, different shapes, colours, and artistic ideas to draw upon later. I know now that I have a very sharp eye – I've always been able to visualise things, and I see and think in visual terms."

This fascinated me. Aitch was describing a deep sensitivity around colour and imagery that I certainly didn't possess, but I could see how it influenced his way of looking at the world, and how it influenced his art.

"My eyes can dance across distance," Aitch continued, "and I take everything in. When I'm driving for example, I'm constantly looking in shop windows, and later on, when I want to buy something, I know exactly where to go to find it, without having consciously registered what I'm doing.

"Art comes in so many forms. It might be in the colour scheme for a Christmas tree or the theme for a dinner party. I've also learnt a lot about colour from the A-list make-up artists I've worked with such as Barbara Daley, and the way they blend different eye shadow colours together. The exposure I've had working closely with them and with top colour technicians and designers over the years has given me so many ideas that I've used in my art."

"How did you start painting?" I asked, curious to find out what had finally stimulated all these influences into creative expression.

"I first started painting about fifteen years ago," Aitch replied. "I had the opportunity to collaborate with a designer called Kristopher Robert-Jude, who was a great inspiration to me and later became a dear friend. It was through him that I really took up painting seriously. For decades, I'd been creating sculpture and texture and movement in my hairstyling career, and so it was only natural for that to become the basis of my art – with the addition of brilliant colours of course. It's a natural transition and source of inspiration."

It was fascinating to listen to Aitch talk about his creativity and the sources of his inspiration. He had a gift for visualisation and a real sensitivity to colour and shape, but as he talked about how he worked and the creative processes he went through, I thought about my own latent creativity. Just as it had taken Aitch many years to express his artistic personality in painting, so it had taken me just as long to think seriously about writing.

Aitch had disappeared for a few moments, but he was soon back with his iPad in his hand. "I want to show you my latest piece," he said excitedly, and having found the images he was looking for, handed it over to me. It was the colours that struck me immediately; deep browns and pinks with touches of turquoise, blended in a bold painting made up of separate pieces in distinctive oblong and square shapes.

"I'm painting this for a client of mine," he said proudly. "Each of the ten sections of the piece will be hung in sequence around the walls of his dining room. I've been working on it after work and at the weekends for several months now and I'm pleased to say it's nearly completed."

"Where do you find the energy?" I asked, knowing how difficult I found it to focus on creative work after a hard day's work.

"Well, Jill," he replied, "I have my canvasses and all my paints laid out on my dining room table, and once I get started I find it relaxing and quite therapeutic. Once I put Classic FM on the radio, I find I can work for hours, and I often paint into the early hours of the morning. The trick is in the preparation. I spend a lot of time working out the shape, the colours and the textures of the painting, and how I'm going to place them together before I start work on my canvas. There's a creative process that I go through in painstaking detail. I know that once I've done my preparation, I'll have a clear vision of the painting in my mind – how it will look and what it will take to complete. With that vision in my head, the creative juices flow naturally. In fact, when I've been going through difficult times I find painting a great source of comfort and pleasure. So I don't find it tiring; it energises me."

I looked at the images of Aitch's latest creation on the iPad in front of me again. I could tell that it would look stunning, hung carefully to accentuate the geometric lines of the canvas shapes and to reflect the light from its colours and textures.

"How do you create those amazing effects?" I asked him.

"The quality and finish of my work is really important," Aitch replied. "I layer acrylic paints and put canvas on canvas with added resin, using marouflage techniques and strong texturing. My signature style is bold abstract shapes in juxtaposition with vibrant colours to create an overall sense of well-being and joie de vivre."

It was an interesting expression – joie de vivre – and immediately reminded me of Aitch's stories about Ben. It was this spirit that had attracted them to each other in the first place, and now Aitch was breathing Ben's spirit into his art. Whoever was going to own this latest painting was, I felt sure, going to enjoy the uplifting effect it would have, and the sense of well-being it would inspire.

There was no more time to explore the topic further and Aitch's attention had already turned to his next client. As I put on my coat and paid my bill, my thoughts turned to my own creative ambitions. Seeing Aitch's work, and the pleasure it clearly gave him, was all the inspiration I could ask for.

Let us be grateful to the people who make us happy as they are the charming gardeners who make our souls bloom.

Marcel Proust

HOMAGE

I was busily going about my business when I heard the news – Vidal Sassoon had died in Los Angeles at the age of eighty-four surrounded by his family. I stopped in my tracks. Aitch had mentioned to me that Vidal had been ill for some time, and I knew he was worried about him, but I wasn't expecting this, especially today – the anniversary of my own father's death. My thoughts immediately turned to Aitch, and how he must be feeling. I sent him a text message, and reflected on the new significance of the date in our respective lives. It seemed to me that Vidal was the high priest of mentors to Aitch; someone who'd believed in him and recognised his talent in the early years as a creative director with huge potential.

Aitch had worked for Vidal and the Sassoon organisation for forty years. They'd experienced a lot together, and seen many changes in their profession over the years. Yet despite retiring some time ago, Vidal was still held in huge esteem. That much was clear from the tributes that came pouring in from around the world as soon as the news of his death broke. He was an icon of the '60s, and he'd transformed the hairdressing industry with his bold and innovative approach.

The next day I read the newspapers avidly and Vidal's picture shone out from all the front pages. The glowing headlines referred to him as an industry legend, a visionary and creative genius, and accredited him with revolutionising the salon industry with his ready-to-wear cuts. Vidal had touched many lives; it was clear that the people who'd had the privilege of working with him viewed him as their mentor, and were deeply grateful for everything they'd learnt from him. As I read the tributes, I knew that Aitch would be feeling desperately sad.

I went up to the Sassoon salon in the City a few days later, taking some white roses with me. I felt somehow it was the right thing to do, and I wanted Aitch to know that I understood his grief. I knew that Vidal's death would bring back many memories – bittersweet in many ways – and they'd remind Aitch of so many things they'd done together. Aitch was unsurprisingly in a sober mood and we didn't talk much, but we embraced and I held him tightly to show I cared.

All of a sudden Vidal Sassoon was big news, and with my new interest in the craft of hairdressing, I was fascinated to see what else I could learn about the man. I went to an exhibition at Somerset House celebrating his career, where there were photos and quotations from him displayed on storyboards. 'Hair is nature's biggest compliment,' he'd written, 'and the treatment of this compliment is in our hands.' Another quote I really liked read, 'Hair cutting simply means: Design. And this feeling for design must come from within.'

Vidal had a way of saying things in a way that suggested a deeper interest in words and culture that surprised me a bit. But I remembered Aitch mentioning to me once that it was Vidal who'd first introduced him to the work of Marcel Proust.

I saw Aitch again a while later just after he'd attended the memorial service that had been held for Vidal in St Paul's Cathedral. He'd taken the day off to make sure he could pay his respects properly and I knew it would have been a day of great emotional significance for him.

"How did it go?" I asked, as sensitively as I could.

"It was a lovely day, thank you, Jill," he said, and I relaxed as he started to tell me all about it.

"I decided to wear my grey tailored morning suit with a grey Prada tie, and I felt very comfortable, even though I was emotional under the surface," Aitch began. "I wanted to do Vidal proud, to look good, to hold my head high and to pay my respects with dignity and poise. The memorial service started at eleven o'clock, but I went to the salon first and met up with a load of old colleagues who were all gathering there. It seemed the most natural place in the world to get together and to reminisce about Vidal and the old days.

"Despite the very sad circumstances, there was a real buzz in the air. There were mobile phones ringing all over the place, lots of 'hello darlings', air kisses and laughter. People arrived from other salons and from the academies and, of course, a lot of them had made a point of getting there early to do their hair – we all wanted to look our very best.

"There was an underlying sadness, of course, but in many ways it was like a big reunion party. Once we'd checked each other out, and everyone was happy with how they looked, we walked up to the cathedral steps and went into St Paul's together. The streets were full of people – workers and tourists as well as the paparazzi – and we felt like minor celebrities. Most importantly, though, it was a moment of respect and reflection – a time to pay homage.

"We were told we had to be in our seats by ten thirty," Aitch continued, "and the ushers took each of us to our places with quiet dignity. St Paul's was looking magnificent, and the grandeur of it all created a wonderful mood. The seating was tiered, with close family and friends at the front, invited guests behind them, and then seats for the public behind that. I was privileged to be sitting three rows behind the family next to Mark Hayes, the International Creative Director and his wife Tracey.

Mark was my young assistant back in the '70s and he's risen since then to the very top of Sassoon. He's extremely talented and I always knew he'd go far. He's one of those people with an easy charm that enables him to engage with clients and staff alike. He was a favourite of Vidal, and he's always been really good at encouraging others – just like Vidal.

"There was a solemn pause before the service began," Aitch continued, "and I knew everyone was desperately hoping their mobile phones wouldn't go off just at that moment. As I sat there in quiet contemplation, I thought of Vidal and all the things we'd done together. I remembered the time we were in the Philippines on the anniversary tour. We'd met royalty and were feted from start to finish, but on one particular day we had some spare time and we decided to go to St Augustine's Cathedral in Manila. He and I stood alongside each other in quiet reflection there, and despite being from a different faith, Vidal made a generous donation to the restoration of the church. That generosity was a sign to me of his belief in equality – and of his supreme serenity, a serenity that I felt descended on St Paul's Cathedral in his honour."

Another stylist came up at the moment, and Aitch excused himself to talk to another client. It was a timely interruption at a poignant moment, and I sat back and reflected on the warmth of Aitch's feelings towards Vidal and his memory. Then he returned and picked up the story without prompting.

"The way the seating was laid out was almost gladiatorial," Aitch continued. "It was like an arena and gave me the opportunity to cast my eyes around and see who else was there. It really was quite a throwback – seeing all those people again that I'd known and worked with in the past. Mary Quant was there, of course – she was always a good friend of Vidal – and Zandra Rhodes was there too, together with Felicity Green who was the managing director of Vidal Sassoon for a long time.

"Then, when everyone was assembled, the service began. The director and producer David Puttnam and the actor Jeremy Irons both gave readings before Vidal's son Elan got to his feet to deliver the eulogy. His words brought everyone to tears, and you could tell from the atmosphere that he'd moved the whole congregation. Then the choir started singing and the music was divine.

"In a way," Aitch said, looking at me with a slightly pained expression, "it all finished too quickly. The service, with all the memories it stirred, had taken me back to a different era and I wanted to linger there a bit longer. We were ushered out of the cathedral once the formalities were over and I emerged into the daylight. I stood on the steps of the cathedral for a few moments feeling nostalgic and emotional."

"What did you do next?" I asked, imagining the mix of emotions and sense of loss Aitch must have been feeling.

"I went out for lunch with Henry Abell and his wife Sally," Aitch said, in a lighter mood. "They're both absolutely charming. Henry used to be the creative director at the Sloane Street salon, and we've stayed friends over the years. He taught me a great deal and is one of the nicest people I know. Over lunch, we talked about the old days when creativity really mattered, and when there was fierce competition about who could do the best haircut, and it made you feel alive. But there was also a real spirit of kinship in the industry."

Aitch paused and I could see that our conversation was having a real effect on him. I hoped that it helped him to talk and that he wasn't feeling too down about the past.

Before I had the chance to ask, Aitch continued with his story. "I was exhausted by the time I got home," he said. "It felt like a very long day, but it was the emotional experience that had affected me. Going to the service helped me reflect on so many things, but I will always regret that I'd didn't have the chance of one last conversation with Vidal. I would have reminded him that I'd worked for Sassoon for forty years, and told him what that meant to me. And I would have told him how grateful I was for the support and friendship he'd given me over the years."

By now, I could feel tears welling up in my eyes, and we consciously avoided looking at each other in the mirror. After completing the rest of my haircut in silence, Aitch looked at me in the mirror. The mood had altered and he was back to his normal self. I could tell he had something else to tell me before I went. I returned his gaze in curious anticipation.

"Later on that day," he said with a smile, "I sent a text to Elan telling him what a great job he'd done – how touching and memorable his words had been to me and everyone else at the service. I've known Elan all his life. I can still picture him as a young boy, but there he was, a grown man giving a moving eulogy at his father's memorial service."

"Did he reply?" I asked, wondering what was coming next.

"For sure," said Aitch, grinning broadly as he recalled their exchange. "He thanked me for my kind words, and then he went on to remind me of a particularly memorable occasion when we went shopping together years and years ago." Aitch paused for effect, but I knew he couldn't wait to tell me why the experience had stuck in Elan's mind for so long. As if about to burst, he bent down to whisper in my ear, "It was the shopping trip when I ended up buying tiger skin patent underwear!"

We both laughed out loud. Aitch had done it again. I was leaving the salon not only with a touching insight into the memorial service of a legend in the world of hairdressing, but with a huge grin on my face.

Your stay on this planet is inescapably brief;
but the manifestations of life are infinite. In
fact, they are so extraordinary, so exciting and
so rich, that your curiosity will be perpetually
provoked by them.

Villiers David,
    Advice to my Godchildren

FULL CIRCLE

I looked myself up and down in the mirror and felt surprisingly good about what I saw in my reflection. My hair was definitely edgier in style and Aitch had even succeeded in getting me to use hair gel to create a more interesting, less coiffured look. He'd also had a subtle influence on how I dressed. The black and navy business suits were now firmly at the back of the wardrobe, and I was experimenting with a younger, more fashionable look. I glanced down at my feet in my first pair of converse sneakers and smiled to myself. *What a long way I'd come.*

I'd recently bought myself a Mini, having not driven a car for years. All the time I was working, there was no real need to drive anywhere as I was either on the tube to the City, or on a plane for a business trip. I expected to be a little anxious driving to Harlesden from my home in Chiswick, but I knew it wasn't just the driving I was nervous about. I was going to visit Aitch for the first time at his home, and it felt like a really significant moment for us both.

Having talked so many times in the salon, we were now entering a new phase in our relationship. For me, it was a sign of the change that I was going through, from being a corporate workhorse with a punishing schedule, to a new more liberated and creative lifestyle.

Despite my nerves I was excited, not least about the small gift I had for Aitch in my bag. Unbeknown to him, I'd tracked down a first edition of Villiers David's book *Advice to my Godchildren*. I'd found it on the Internet and ordered it from an obscure little bookshop in New York. When the parcel finally arrived, it was tiny and at first I thought I'd been fleeced. But when I carefully peeled off the wrapping, I found a slim but beautifully presented book published in 1951. It had an inscription inside, 'To Sarah and Tom, this is number one on my list for basic library volumes in homes of distinction, Brock'.

The book was only thirty-two pages long, so it didn't take long to read from cover to cover, but it made sense of so many things. It was the philosophy that Aitch had lived his life by, without him ever having read the book for himself. So much of who he was had come from the lessons Ben had taught him from his own reading of Villiers David. I knew that Aitch would be thrilled to see the book, and I couldn't wait to show him.

As I followed signs to Harlesden while driving through Shepherd's Bush and White City, I had a sense of coming full circle. I was watching carefully where I was going as I wasn't familiar with the route, but I knew that once I reached Harlesden, (or 'da hood' as Aitch liked to call it), it would be strangely familiar. My mother was born in Harlesden and in her younger days had lived just around the corner from where Aitch lived. So in a way, it felt like a homecoming. When I was a child, we used to visit this part of London regularly to see family. Here I was, back again in Harlesden, nearly fifty years later. It was a connection with Aitch that neither of us could have imagined when we first met.

I parked my car outside Aitch's flat and took a deep breath. I was anxious about how our conversation would go as we'd only ever spoken in the salon up to then. And I was nervous about whether I really could write Aitch's story. It was going to be quite a test for both of us. Aitch had offered to make lunch and I'd brought along some cheese and chocolates. I grabbed them, walked up to his front door, and rang the bell.

In a matter of seconds, Aitch was beaming at me in the doorway. He gave me a big hug smelling as gorgeous as usual. He was dressed more casually than I had ever seen him before, but he still managed to look stylish, and held himself like a principal ballerina. His white linen trousers skimmed his hips and his shirt was loose and flowing. I looked down at his feet, spotted his Converse trainers, and felt a sense of sartorial kinship.

As we went up the stairs to his flat, I was amused to see spotlights on either side of each step – it gave a touch of glamour to the place and I felt like I was entering the home of a celebrity. I walked into the hallway with the sunshine streaming through the windows and I could see a roof garden on the balcony leading off the dining room, with a pretty water feature, a sun lounger, and what looked like real grass.

Aitch was as determined as ever to put me at ease, and instinctively understood how I might be feeling. He invited me to sit down while he made coffee and talked about his morning to bring a sense of normality to our encounter. As I did so, I noticed a well-thumbed book on the table. *Daily Meditations for People of Color*, it was called, by Iyania Vanzant. I picked it up and started to flick through it. Each page had a quotation and a short reflection on life for every day of the year. I glanced at one or two of them and was surprised at how insightful they were. I could tell that Aitch read one every day. He saw me looking at the book and called out from the kitchen, "that was given to me as a birthday present many years ago by Colin, a very good friend of mine." I put the book down after a few minutes and looked around the room.

There was a beautiful white fitted cabinet with etched glass doors and blue down-lighters that showed off an expansive glass collection, just like the one his grandmother had had I imagined. On the large glass dining room table were tiny vases each holding a single white rosebud and small mounds of wax from candles that had spilled over. Around the table were silver-coloured dining chairs with seats in bright purple, pink, turquoise and ochre stripes.

Aitch's own paintings adorned the pristine white walls and their vivid colours, textures and shapes defined the room as that of an artist. I'd only seen one of Aitch's paintings up close before in the salon. Sitting in his dining room surrounded by his work made me realise what an accomplished artist he was.

Once the coffee was made, Aitch led me into his sitting room. It was a large room with a high ceiling and sash windows, and it was bathed in light. In the centre was a square glass coffee table strewn with books on art and design. There were lots of framed photos of his family and friends, and too many objets d'art for me to take in all at once. I noticed the candles placed around the fireplace and on the mantelpiece, and I remembered Aitch's story about going to church as a young boy in Dominica, and how he'd always loved candles and the soft light they create. These candles were expensive ones with exotic scents, and were clearly well used.

At either side of the room, there were two magnificent ivory white chaise longues with elegant tassels and embroidered cushions. I thought of the description of Ben's stylish flat in Cadogan Gardens, and of the fabulous designer homes he'd had the privilege to see in Los Angeles and I could see the influences stamped firmly on the design of the room. It might be a flat in 'da hood' but Aitch had made it a stylishly chic place to live. I could see how Aitch's natural curiosity, his ability to observe and his keen eye for detail, had all played a part in putting the final touches to his taste and flavours in everything from the furnishings of his flat to his own artwork.

We sat down and I took a sip of the coffee that Aitch had made me for me. He was always very particular about his coffee and it was unsurprisingly delicious. We started to talk.

Before long, it felt just like one of our conversations in the salon and I knew that everything was going to be alright. In fact, we had so much to talk about that any worries I had about material quickly disappeared. It was more a question of how I could do justice to his colourful life. It made me realise how much trust had developed between us.

Despite our differences, we had a strong mutual respect. I'd learnt so much from Aitch about his craft, about art and ballet and opera, and I really admired the way he'd followed his natural curiosity with determination and discretion to broaden his horizons. I reflected on the fact that curiosity was also one of my own strong characteristics, and that Aitch and I shared a desire to enhance our lives by having many different experiences.

It was an epiphany moment. I'd been wondering where the connection between us really lay, why it was that I of all people had ended up at his home on a Saturday morning discussing writing a book about him over coffee. And now I knew. We shared a curiosity about the world, a determination to learn our craft, and to be creative and professional at the same time.

After a couple of hours talking about our project, we took a break and Aitch finished preparing lunch. The smells from the kitchen had started to be a distraction to my concentration; the wonderful aromas of different spices and herbs made me feel quite hungry. I freshened up in the bathroom while Aitch was busy in the kitchen.

As I'd expected, the bathroom had every bit of Aitch's style. There was a black marble sink with expensive black soap and tiny spotlights around the mirror above it. On the shelf was a full range of Esencia for men. I picked up a beautiful emerald green glass bottle that had a gold cap and the brand name Loewe embossed in leather, and held it under my nose – it was Aitch's signature smell, the fragrance he wore every day, and which identified him instantly.

It was an informal lunch, but it was prepared with love and with style. Aitch produced a starter of smoked salmon with lemon covered in thin muslin, served on pink Villeroy and Boch china plates and set on huge silver platters. I felt completely spoilt. The main course arrived next. It was a special Caribbean recipe of salted fish that he'd marinated overnight in spices and herbs, and that he served with sweet potatoes, stuffed courgette and rice, all beautifully presented just as I could have predicted. The table was dressed with a white tablecloth, linen napkins and inscribed silver napkin rings.

I sat back and smiled as Aitch poured a red juice into a long-stemmed purple glass goblet.

"What's this?" I asked curiously.

"It's sorrel juice," said Aitch, "made from a flower like a thistle. My sister made it as part of the business she's setting up."

I took a sip and it was truly delicious, just like nectar from the Caribbean. We clinked our goblets together, and made a toast to our project.

"Before we get started in earnest," I said, "there is one thing I want to ask you."

"For sure," said Aitch "what do you want to know?"

"Well," I said, suddenly feeling a little shy, "where does the name Aitch come from?" He roared with laughter. Aitch had had no idea that this question was on my mind; he was, of course, so familiar with his own name that it never occurred to him to explain it to anyone.

"Well, it's certainly not the name I was born with, Jill," he confessed. "I was christened Hensworth Francis Lestrade Peters, would you believe, or Haines for short. But being known as Aitch goes right back to my time with Ben. The first gift he bought me was a wonderful leather Hermès belt with a huge shining buckle in the shape of the letter 'H'. I fell in love with it, and before long, the Hermès signature became my brand, spelt A-I-T-C-H.

"Of course, it's also the first letter of my real name and it does get a bit confusing at times. Lots of people get mixed up and end up referring to me as Henry or Harry, but it's only my family who still refer to me by my real name. Although Donald has been known to call me Haines," he added, "when he's joking me – or coming over all unnecessary." He let out one of his deep raucous laughs, and I couldn't help but smile.

So at last I knew the ultimate mystery about Aitch – the source of his identity. How fitting that it should come from those formative years with Ben. I felt like I'd been taken into a secret place. The name made absolute sense to me. It symbolised who he was. We ended up talking and laughing for hours – or rather Aitch did most of the talking and I did my best to capture it all. He was thrilled to have a copy of Villiers David's book at last. He held it carefully in his hands and turned it over and over before carefully opening the pages and starting to read the words. He looked up at me over his glasses, and we both knew the book would always have a special place in his heart.

When I got home, I dug out my copy of Vidal Sassoon's autobiography again. I wanted to remind myself of some of those profound statements he'd made. I fell upon one particular quotation that summed up everything perfectly when I thought about Aitch, his life, and the impact he'd had on me. This was it: 'When everybody tells you – the doubters tell you – it can't be done, you'll grow broke or all kinds of tragedies will come your way: Nonsense. If you can get to the root of who you are, the guts of who you are, and make something happen from it – in whatever field – my sense is you're going to surprise yourself.'

I went into my study and sat down in front of the screen. I typed out the first word: A-I-T-C-H. The story was underway. As I started writing, I had a feeling that Vidal would be very proud of us, of Aitch and me – a most unlikely couple.

ACKNOWLEDGEMENTS

I'd often said that one day I wanted to write a book, and there came a point when I just had to see if I could. After a long career in the City, I was ready for a change of direction, and keen to exercise my creativity that I felt had been stifled by decades spent in corporate life. Then I met Aitch and he gave me the inspiration I needed to get started. Working with Aitch has been a real pleasure, and my thanks are first and foremost to him – for his candidness and openness about the ups and downs in his life, his honesty about his true feelings, and of course, for all those wonderful haircuts.

Over the course of a year or so, we would meet in his flat in Harlesden and he would tell me more of his stories and make me laugh – all while cooking me a most delicious lunch. We really are a most unlikely couple, but we discovered a deep and mutual respect for each other that underpins the writing of this book.

Thanks are also due to my husband Mike, who has been a great support in my new career, and to my mum for always being so proud of me. Finally, there's my own personal book club, a circle of girlfriends who've listened patiently to my plans and my progress, who've taken an enthusiastic interest in the project, and offered ideas and views along the way: Phil, Sarah, Jo, Rhona, Karen, Lesley, Sally, Libby, Anna, Fenella, Val and Barbara – a big thank you to you all for your encouragement, and for your friendship.

Jill King

Acknowledgements

Phillip Rogers

Andrew Corlett
Darryl Hope
Steve Jolson
John Roberts
Kristopher Robert-Jude
Donald Walsh
Caryn Franklin
Edward Daley
Chris Fields
Mark Hayes
Susie Mutch and her team
All Sassoon Salon Directors and the Creative team
The formidable team at the City salon headed by Stuart Lloyd
All the salon receptionists, stylists, technicians and assistants I've
worked with
All my clients over the years

A Massive Thanks To You All for your Special Support

Kristof Pacura – Cover photos and photo editing

Swizzlestick: Info@swizzle-stick.co.uk
Gee@Gee Barbers Kensal Rise
Ali@ Perfect Dry Cleaners

Aitch Peters

A big thank you to Jill King
YOU ARE A STAR
This would not have been possible without your vision,
passion, sensitivity and penmanship

Donald Hill
Thank you for your Love, Support and Encouragement
I love you, Aitch xxx

And finally,
To my dear mother Linda and all my family
I love you
Aitch xxx

AITCH: A CAREER IN HIGHLIGHTS

Aitch Peters has spent over 35 years with Sassoon in London, Munich and Los Angeles where he was Creative Director of the Beverly Hills salon for many years. He is now in residence at the Sassoon salon in the City of London where he works with a great team and attends to his many loyal clients who have supported his rise to the sought after stylist and accomplished Artist that he is today.

Aitch's career started the day he first walked through the doors of the Sassoon Academy back in 1973. Since then his knowledge and wide ranging experience have made him a unique asset to the Sassoon brand.

Over the course of his career he has worked with leading photographers including:

- Richard Avedon
- David Bailey
- Gary Bernstein
- Terence Donovan
- Barry Lategan
- Annie Leibovitz
- Lord Lichfield
- Terry O'Neill
- Lord Snowdon
- Mario Testino

He has seen his work credited in the major international fashion magazines including:

- Italian Vogue
- UK Vogue
- Harpers & Queen
- Tatler magazine
- Essence
- The Hollywood Reporter
- Black Elegance

He has worked with up and coming designers at Fashion Colleges, Art schools and Degree shows including:

- The London College of Fashion
- Otis Art Institute/Parsons School of Design, L.A.
- Saint Martin's School of Art and Design
- The Royal College of Art

He has worked on well-known US TV shows including:

- The Johnny Carson Show
- The Merv Griffin Show
- The Debbie Allen Special
- Eye on L.A.
- A Different World

And Aitch feels privileged to have worked with numerous celebrities including:

- Saffron Burrows
- Nicolas Cage
- Mariah Carey

- André Cymone
- Faye Dunaway
- The First Lady of the Philippines
- Whoopi Goldberg
- Jerry Hall
- Iman
- The Reverend Jesse Jackson
- Annie Lennox
- Matthew Modine
- Lorraine Pascale
- Ruth Pointer
- Gordon Ramsey
- Tracey Ullman
- Jody Watley